OUR BOYS

Richard Aston is the CEO of Big Buddy, Chairman of Consumer NZ and an independent marriage celebrant. Ruth Kerr is the Media Coordinator at Big Buddy and a freelance journalist. They have been married for 30 years and have a number of children and grandchildren.

Big Buddy is a free, secular mentoring service run by dedicated professionals who recruit and rigorously screen male volunteers from the community to become mentors to fatherless boys.

Ruth Kerr & Richard Aston

OUR BOYS

Raising strong, happy sons from boyhood to manhood

ALLEN&UNWIN
SYDNEY•MELBOURNE•AUCKLAND•LONDON

First published in 2016

Allen & Unwin
Level 3, 228 Queen Street
Auckland 1010, New Zealand
Phone: (64 9) 377 3800

Email: info@allenandunwin.com
Web: www.allenandunwin.co.nz

83 Alexander Street
Crows Nest NSW 2065, Australia
Phone: (61 2) 8425 0100

A catalogue record for this book is available
from the National Library of New Zealand

ISBN 978 1 87750 552 2

Set in 12/18 pt Adobe Garamond by Midland Typesetters, Australia
Printed and bound in Australia by Griffin Press

10 9 8 7 6 5 4 3 2 1

MIX
Paper from
responsible sources
FSC
www.fsc.org   FSC® C009448

The paper in this book is FSC® certified.
FSC® promotes environmentally responsible,
socially beneficial and economically viable
management of the world's forests.

We dedicate Our Boys *to the memory of passionate boys'
advocate Celia Lashlie (10 June 1953–16 February 2015).*

*Her advice to mothers to 'get off the bridge' and allow boys
to grow up through experiencing risk was radical
but right—someone needed to say it and
that someone was Celia.*

*She reminded us that our boys are more than the sum of
the 'problems' we label them with: they are gorgeous—
creative, fun, adventurous and capable of great depth.*

*Thank you for your courage and passion, Celia, and know
that the work goes on. This one's for you.*

Contents

Introduction

Charlie (4 years): 'Mum, can ants do forward flips?'

Mum: 'I don't think so, Charlie.'

Charlie: 'I think professional ants can.'

Congratulations—it's a boy!

Parenting has got to be the hardest gig of all. There's nothing more satisfying when it goes well and nothing more heart-breaking when it comes unstuck.

You'll feel love for your kids that surpasses every other emotion known to humankind. You'll also feel anguish and despair that has no equal and will undo you, time and time again. Whoever said 'We're only ever as happy as our saddest child' was bang on the money. Welcome to the *big* love!

The first thing we want to say is that we're not parenting experts. We're just in the fortunate position of having raised four pretty wonderful kids in a blended family and made enough mistakes over many years to offer you our wisdom. Our kids will verify this!

But, hopefully, some of our advice on raising boys resonates with you as you navigate the pothole-ridden path of parenting. Because what we can tell you is that it's a roller-coaster that will take you on the biggest journey of your life. You'll learn more about yourself than you ever imagined, and not all of it will be pleasant. Thank goodness for therapists!

What we hope the take-away message from this book will be is that, time after time, parenting is about 'leaning in'. If you're not familiar with this expression, it means to really engage—to face into things and, when it gets tough, to face in even more.

Like us, you'll stuff up in ways you never thought possible, and be served curveballs only a sci-fi writer could ever dream up! The trick is to get up, dust yourself off, look the situation squarely in the eye, learn what you can from it, apologise if you need to and move on, knowing you'll handle it differently next time. Forgive yourself for being an oaf; for not knowing what you didn't know—hell, if you'd had more skills, you wouldn't have unleashed the dogs of hell in your own living room!

Then there will be the sweet times that will sustain and feed you. You'll watch your boy emerge into a fine young man and the love and energy you've poured into him will shine through. He'll fill your heart with pride and joy as he sets about carving out his adult life in ways you never imagined. He will amaze you! You'll be able to sit back some, relaxed in the knowledge he stands on good foundations that will serve him—and his children—well. Hold onto this image, people!

In this book, we've focused on raising boys because that's what we know quite a bit about. Since 2003, we've been involved in the work of Big Buddy—a mentoring organisation that has matched over 650 fatherless boys with well-screened male mentors. In the course of vetting many hundreds of volunteer male mentors, we've learned a lot about what shapes men's lives. We've also followed the trajectories of our Little Buddies—the boys who are mentored—over a 13-year period. This work has provided a rich seam of knowledge about what boys need to become good men—men with good moral compasses, who won't always do the right thing but will know when they've stuffed up, and learn from it. Men with emotional intelligence.

We also think boys are in a spot of bother. Their lives have changed radically, particularly over the last 50 to 60 years as technology has gained a big foothold on the human story. That wonderful entertainer television, introduced to the masses in the early 1950s, reached New Zealand homes in 1960. We gradually spent less time in the great outdoors and more time on the couch laughing at sitcoms that parodied men and portrayed them as gormless, blundering, emotional retardees. A cynic would say they then set about becoming just that!

Home computers followed the arrival of TV some 20 years later, leading us even further into the highly digital and sedentary world we now inhabit. Fantastic as this world is—expanding both our girths and our cerebral horizons beyond our wildest dreams—it hasn't necessarily worked out so well for our boys.

In fact, the stats for boys are grim: they are almost twice as likely to be diagnosed with emotional and behavioural problems as girls, New Zealand's youth suicide rate is one of the highest in the OECD, and men commit suicide at a rate of three to one to women. And then there's the disproportionate number of young men who die on our roads—or kill others there.

Boys' educational achievement rates aren't flash either: statistics show that female students outperform their male peers across all three standards—reading, writing and maths. Overall, girls perform better in all school qualifications except Scholarship, where boys catch up. Then women charge ahead again at university, outnumbering men in the graduation stakes in almost every age category. Maori and Pasifika boys fare even worse.

And brace yourself for the crime stats: as in many countries, the vast majority of crime in New Zealand is committed by males. In 2014, police apprehended just under 33,000 females, compared to 122,800 males—a ratio of 1 to 3.72. At the end of December 2014, there were 8080 male prisoners in New Zealand jails, compared to 561 women inmates.

Crikey, you may well be thinking—what's gone wrong here? Isn't this supposed to be the 'greatest country in the world to bring up kids'? Well, yes—and no. We know the problems are not ours alone—most countries in the developed world share these type of statistics. So what's gone so wrong for boys?

Social scientists are still wrestling with this one but we suspect the problem lies in the transition from a mechanical into a digital age that hasn't taken account of the biggest male driver of all—testosterone. Boys experience surges of this hormone throughout their childhoods until the final big whammy hits, plunging them into puberty at around the age of 14. Women have it as well, of course, but testosterone levels are 10 times higher in men—it's the 'activity hormone' that controls growth, risk-taking, physical courage, strength, speed and aggression. It's what makes boys need lots of physical activity and drives them to take risks, and it's what limits both their empathy and their ability to weigh up cause and effect when it's blindingly obvious to the rest of us. It's not called the 'bad boy' driver for nothing!

Maybe boys' testosterone levels will eventually decrease, in an evolutionary drift better reflecting our more sedentary lifestyles, but until then we have to do something about our boys. We have to figure out better ways to educate them, stop them killing themselves and others, and help more of them transition into manhood in healthier ways, so they can be both happier and lead more fulfilling lives. To be the best men they can be.

The challenges ahead of us all are immense in terms of issues like territorial boundaries, social equity, health, housing, resource and waste management, urban design and climate change, and it will take inspired, creative young people to find solutions to them. We need our courageous boys to contribute to this crucial change culture—not be cut off at the knees by attitudes and systems that don't work to their strengths or encourage them to reach their potential. We owe them that.

Neuroscientists have known for years that the brains of men and women are not identical. There is good evidence now that testosterone plays a significant role in the trajectory of boys' brain development, which is hugely different from girls—their cognitive brain continues to form up to the age of around 25 to 26, whereas in girls it's done by 19 to 20. So raising boys is an entirely different process from raising girls.

Of course, hormone levels vary between individuals, with some boys having more testosterone than others (this is true for girls as well). But generally speaking, most boys sit somewhere at the stronger testosterone end of the spectrum, and most girls will sit at the lower. How they are influenced by the 'bad boy' driver will depend on a number of biological and cultural factors.

From birth, our kids are exposed to many ideas and attitudes that influence their social behaviour regarding gender roles, from parents, siblings, peers, and more. It's difficult to tease apart which behaviours and attitudes are inherent and which are socialised, because gender stereotypes are so pervasive, particularly in the media. The fear is, of course, that gender stereotypes limit people's choices and create inequality. And none of us want that. In the end we can only work off our experiences of gender differences and use them as a guide, without locking kids into stereotypes that limit and potentially harm them.

Having said that, our position is that generally speaking, boys are different from girls, and that parenting them requires a different approach—particularly around their physical and emotional needs. This is based on our experiences of many hundreds of mothers asking us to find mentors for their fatherless boys, because despite them doing everything they can to help their boys grow into good men, they 'sense something is missing' from their boys' lives. They believe that missing 'something' is a good man. We agree. While women do a brilliant and courageous job raising boys alone, they cannot model maleness. And above all else, boys learn to become men through modelling.

We believe maleness is caught, not taught, and that it's time for men to shuck off the ridiculous TV identities foisted on them and reclaim their place as fathers and mentors to their boys. It's time for them to confidently model what it is to be a good-hearted man.

The truth is, raising boys is no great mystery—after all, we have been doing it for hundreds of thousands of years—but raising well-rounded, healthy men with strong foundations is a whole other story. The strongest message we can give is that this is not a manual telling you what to *do* as you raise your boys—it's more advice on how to *be* around them and, more importantly, alongside them.

The most frequent question we get from mothers is, 'What sort of man will my boy become?' It's a question loaded with hopes and fears.

It is also a valid question that you can use to guide your parenting style, making you the type of parent you are growing in to. Because that's the rub—you're always *becoming* a good parent; it's a lifelong journey that involves getting to know yourself through engaging in your children's development. Being mindful of your own thoughts, fears, expectations and projections is, we think, one of the most important competencies a parent should grow.

When you become a parent, the first thing you need to do is reflect on your own parents, because fight it as you may, your parenting will be driven by how you were parented. If you're not conscious of this, your parenting will be controlled by it. Ultimately, parenting is about who you are as much as it is about what you do or say. This is especially true in the early years.

Having a child is going to bring up some personal stuff for you, and your ability to front up to your own issues will make a power of difference to your son. Because boys are like sponges, taking in everything around them with built-in antennae, especially from those who love and care for them. As they grow older, their antennae becomes like a satellite dish—seeking out and searching for the masculine; a finely tuned radar receiving all the masculine stuff out there, trying to make sense of it and integrating it into a boy's own sense of what it means to be male.

At a fundamental level, children need air, water, food, clothing, shelter, to be emotionally attached, kept safe from accidents, cared for when they're sick, to feel affection and to be held and cuddled.

At this primary level of need, there is really no difference between boys and girls, aside, perhaps, from some minor matters of style. It's as they begin the journey through boyhood into becoming men that boys need more—more engagement, more physical interaction, more praise and more real-life heroes they can pin their aspirations on. Our advice to you—especially fathers—is to try to be one of those people.

Finally, our greatest hope is not only that this book helps you *survive* parenting your boys, but enables you to really enjoy them. Because boys are creative, energetic, fun, often left-field thinkers who will entertain and challenge you in equal measure. Enjoy the ride! Kia kaha, fellow travellers.

ONE

Hush little baby: the first four years

> How you speak to your children becomes their inner voice.
>
> Mike King, comedian and creator of 'The Nutters Club'

The one thing we truly know about parenting is that children learn from who you are—both mother and father—not from what you tell them. They are tuning in to who you are and how you operate in the world, almost from conception. Our daughter says when she was pregnant and her partner came home from work and started talking, her baby would go crazy in utero—that child absolutely differentiated between his father's and other voices while still in the womb. It's a different voice; a deep voice—different from Mum's.

So you are, in our opinion, the biggest single teacher your children will have. Meeting their basic needs of feeding, burping, changing, settling, etc., is relatively easy from birth to the age of about three—it's the 'how' you go about caring for them that makes the deepest impact.

The 'how' you are in the world is determined by your own upbringing and experiences, and the more you reflect on and understand the drivers in your own life, the more likely you are to be the parent you want to be. You'll be much less likely to project your unprocessed stuff onto your boy.

If, for example, you're conscious of the effects of not being praised, or of not having a father in your life, you will be able to not project that onto your boy—you'll be able to be empathetic to his unique needs. You won't need him to be a mini-me—becoming the rock legend or rugby player you wished you could have been. Instead, you'll see what's emerging out of him and nurture that. That takes curiosity and a willingness to be surprised; sure, there will be lots of chips off the old block that connect your son back to you, but he will be forming up his own unique block too—watch and be amazed!

Because the human brain isn't fully formed until about the age of three, up until then it is still gathering information about how it needs to be to operate in the world. It's taking everything in—sucking everything up—as it forms thousands of neural pathways. Is Mum relaxed while she's feeding me? Is Dad's voice harsh? Does he pick me up roughly? Are Mum's eyes kind when she looks at me? Do they respond to me when I cry? Who else is on the scene?

Babies are minutely tuned in to your tone of voice, facial expressions and actions. Because women physically carry babies, the main tuning in is to mothers, and we believe this continues through to between two and three years of age, when gender identity kicks in and boys begin really looking to the men in their lives to form their identity. At around three the development of the individual begins, when a boy starts to wake up to 'I am boy'.

That's not to say fathers don't have a role to play before then—that early bonding will prove critical in the next stages of your boy's development. Fathers can equally participate in most early caring functions, except, of course, breastfeeding. Everything fathers put into the early stages of their child's development will make the next steps so much easier. All the nurturing, the skin-to-skin contact, the engagement—it's gonna be gold when he hits the terrible twos and you become boundary man! (See 'Finding his "No!"' on page 21.)

So, no pressure, folks, but . . . the first three years of your boy's life are critical in shaping who he will become. How you bond with and attach to him in these early years will lay down his social foundations and influence everything from his resilience to the career and relationship choices he makes.

We highly recommend that fathers be at the birth of their children, because that's their best chance of bonding with their baby. We'd go further and say it's essential. The best parents are the ones that are strongly bonded with their children from birth, so dads—be there if you can; cut the cord, have early skin contact. Don't hold back on engagement with your child because you figure his mother knows more than you about nurturing—trust your instincts and blunder in, supporting both your partner and engaging with your child wherever you can. Everyone gets some of it wrong but if you stay tuned to your partner and baby, you'll soon catch on to what works and what doesn't. And hey, she's gonna tell you when you get it wrong anyway!

Research shows that fathers who bond with their children from an early age are much less likely to abuse or neglect them. So early bonding is best for the father and, ultimately, for the child.

If there is no father available or he's not in the picture—regardless of what your situation is—we suggest you think about a good-hearted man in your wider whanau who could take a fatherly role with your boy. It may be a really close friend, an uncle, a cousin or a grandfather . . . if you look, he'll be there. And it may well be that he'll be very honoured to be asked to play a role in your son's life, rather than seeing it as a burden. At Big Buddy we get hundreds of wonderful men stepping up as volunteer mentors to fatherless boys and we see the rich results of these relationships. (See 'Field of fathering' on page 120.)

It's all about attachment

At the end of the day, what you want is to feel a deep, loving attachment to your child—that will do most of the work of parenting. We like to say 'love is a verb'. When you become attached to your child, 'love' becomes 'loving'—love expressed—and that 'love in action' is what we believe sits at the very heart of parenting. It's one thing to say 'I love you' to your child but quite another thing to do the work of loving them—to care for them so deeply that you are compelled to action in relation to loving them.

According to psychologists it's all about attachment. The style or pattern of early attachment a baby has to his parents, particularly his mother—and whether it is secure—will determine his ability to form healthy relationships in the future.

Attachment theory is a work in progress, which originated with British psychologist/psychiatrist John Bowlby's work in the late 1950s and continues to be expanded on by other psychologists. It is based on the premise that the primary provider of food—normally the mother—is the first strong attachment a baby forms. It's not so much about the food as about care and responsiveness—the baby learns trust and safety because the primary caregiver is matching care to the baby's needs. The theory is that this will lay down the foundations for all future relationships—hopefully loving ones—as your baby learns to trust you and his world. He's unlikely to remember these early years but he will know whether or not he felt secure and loved.

The most critical thing your son is learning from birth to the age of four is to give and receive love. When you roll up your sleeves and get involved in his play, the message you give your son is that he's important enough for you to spend time with him—and when he feels important, he feels loved. And when he feels loved . . . well, let's face it, we all do better when we feel loved.

Babies come into the world hard-wired to form attachments because it will ensure their survival. They are scanning their environment—sensing who is most likely to meet their needs, both physically and emotionally.

Remember, the most important thing about forming attachments is not necessarily who feeds and changes the baby but who plays and communicates with him, so dads have a crucial role to play in this early attachment, as well as being the linchpin for helping kids learn about physical boundaries through things like play-fighting from around two onwards.

Studies show that up to three months of age, babies will attach to pretty much anyone who takes care of them. Then they latch onto one primary person between four and nine months, before opening up to other attachments again. That primary person caring for a baby between four and nine months is still generally the mother (presuming your baby is breastfed). We believe this is the most important relationship during this time but there's still plenty fathers can be doing.

Dave Owens, who founded Great Fathers—an organisation dedicated to supporting fathers—says on his website men shouldn't wait until the 'baby period' is over to get involved. 'Men who do that miss out. Children change every day. The greatest thing you can do for your baby is to be right in there with him, as much as you can . . . on his terms, not yours.'

Besides all the basics of feeding, changing, washing, etc., what you can do in these early stages is simple; it's about practical engagement:

- Your baby needs to see your face as much as possible—make lots of eye contact with him; play peek-a-boo-type face games.
- Talk to him—tell him about your day, tell him stories.
- Skin-on-skin contact is good—maybe give him a gentle massage with baby oil.
- Take him for walks and talk/sing to him as you go.
- Read to him—maybe make your own picture books with photos of relatives/friends.
- Establish routines and be consistent.
- Give him 'tummy time'—get down on the floor with him.
- Sing to him.
- Kiss him and blow raspberries on his belly.
- Incorporate him into your exercise routine—do push-ups with him lying below you and make funny faces—he'll laugh his head off!

The important thing is that your boy gets the message he's safe, loved, valued and that his needs will be met—hopefully by you.

So far, so good! How you're going will show up in his 'attachment style'—ranging between *secure* and *insecure*.

Before you roll over in horror at the daunting task of trying to achieve secure attachment for fear of condemning your new baby boy to a life of abject dysfunction, it's important to say that most parents just do the best they can with the skills they have at the time. The fact is, you don't know what you don't know, and unless you've learned some basics about human development, you are unlikely to parent from anything other than instinct—how you were parented is likely to be how you parent, unless you consciously attempt to do it differently.

We think human development should be a core subject at secondary school, given that the vast majority of us will become parents at some stage, responsible for the care and development of children. Honestly, if we'd understood a lot more about how children develop during our kids' early years, we would have done things differently—such as not taking their behaviours so personally. We would have seen 'stages of development' for what they were, instead of sometimes thinking our children were the devil's spawn—hell-bent on driving us crazy!

For example, when we first got together, Richard's four-year-old son started punching—particularly Ruth's three-year-old daughter, his new step-sister—and we didn't know how to deal with it. We were sensitive to the fact that there was a new child living with his father when he didn't, but we also felt incredibly protective of our own children and ended up fighting with each other over it: 'You need to make him stop hitting my daughter!' Our solution? In frustration, we decided Richard would punch him back in a ridiculous and futile effort to teach him not to punch! It was traumatising for everyone and completely pointless. All it illustrates is our lack of parenting skills at the time.

What we didn't understand was that when children become physically aggressive, it's because they haven't developed impulse control like adults have (well, most of them anyway)—we've had to learn to channel the expression of our anger away from physical violence; we've learned to use our words. (See 'Finding his "No!"' on page 21.) This is a cognitive process that takes time and brain development, and the reality for our son was that at four, he simply hadn't matured sufficiently to do anything other than lash out. And he was dealing with big emotions that overwhelmed his developing impulse control.

So, your baby boy is watching everything you do as he strives to make sense of his world. Starting from birth, he's learning who he is by how he is treated. Everyday interactions with parents, relatives and caregivers send him messages such as: you're clever; you're good at figuring things out; you make me laugh; you're loved; I enjoy being with you. These are the messages that will shape your boy's self-esteem.

Between birth and three he's racing through the developmental stages as he learns to roll, crawl, stand, walk and run; to talk, joke, rhyme and sing. He's lifting stuff, dropping things, looking, poking, pouring, bouncing, hiding, tasting, building, knocking down. While he's having fun, he's also learning how to solve problems (such as how much water fills a pot) and discovering all sorts of new concepts, like what floats and what sinks; what bounces and what breaks; what's hard and what's soft. He's engaged in the true work of childhood—play! (See 'Igniting his imagination' on page 28.)

It's important to stress here that not all boys develop in the same way, at the same time. They tick off the developmental stages at their own pace and in their own way, regardless (or sometimes in spite of) your hopes and aspirations for them.

What's important in this play is discovery: your boy discovering the world around him and how he fits into it. We think it's important to allow your boy the scope to explore without trying too hard to 'stimulate' him. The world's an interesting place; let his curiosity, his imagination, lead the way—not yours. It may look chaotic at times but if he's engaged in the play, that's all that matters. Trust that amazing neurological pathways are being forged as he explores his brave new world.

We're talking testosterone

While testosterone levels differ from boy to boy, there is common acceptance that boys are different from girls because of this hormone. You'll notice the differences when you observe boys—particularly ones at the higher end of the testosterone spectrum. They are constantly on the go—climbing, falling, exploring; they'll love things that work—any mechanical devices; they eat simply to refuel and won't give a toss what they wear. At the other end of the spectrum will be the boys who are happy playing quietly; watching the world; maybe dreamy; exploring the inner workings of devices; looking at books; noticing changes of clothes and colours. Most boys will range over the spectrum—happy engaging in both their inner and outer worlds.

But as mentioned earlier, the brains of males and females differ from birth, according to neuroscientists. By three months of age, boys' and girls' brains respond differently to the sound of human speech. This is put down to testosterone, which affects the growth and survival of neurons in some parts of the brain. In men's brains, the two cerebral hemispheres operate more independently during specific mental tasks like speaking or navigating around environments, whereas women tend to use both their hemispheres more equally for the same tasks. Another difference is that males of all ages tend to have slightly larger brains, on average, than females, even allowing for differences in body size. But what does this mean? Well, the boffins are still arguing about it but given that geniuses like Albert Einstein had an average-sized brain, we reckon it's not significant to raising boys.

Testosterone surges occur:

- In your seven-week-old male foetus, when his genitals form.
- Immediately after birth, when the testosterone levels of your baby boy spike at about half the level of an adult male. They will rise fairly significantly between the second and third month, but then begin to fall quickly.
- At about four, when it triggers activity and boyishness. (The occurrence of this surge is contentious, with some research showing that by the time boys are six months old, their testosterone levels are extremely low and stay that way until they approach puberty—see *Stepping out: 4 to 7 years*, page 45.)
- At 13, when you see rapid growth and disorientation.
- At 14, when your boy starts testing the limits and becoming a man.

Hormonal differences mean boys and girls tend to develop in certain areas at different times—girl babies are slightly more advanced in vision, hearing, memory, smell and touch than their male counterparts. And, according to the experts, girl babies generally lead boys in fine-motor and language skills, and are also generally more socially attuned—responding more to human voices and/or faces, or crying more vigorously in response to another baby's cry. It starts early!

But worry not—boys eventually catch up in many of these areas and by the age of three, they tend to outperform girls in visual-spatial integration, which is involved in activities like hand-eye coordination, navigation and doing things like jigsaw puzzles.

The important thing to remember here is just to keep putting opportunities for play in front of your growing boy. Here are some ideas:

- Let him be out in the garden with you.
- Play in the sand and the surf at the beach—don't forget to explore rock pools.
- Take him for walks in the bush and tell him about plants.
- Pull stuff out of the kitchen cupboards and let him play on the floor or outside.
- Let him make mud cakes in the garden and help him decorate them.
- Build a hill out of leaves or lawn clippings and hide in them.
- Make a tent under the kitchen table and have a picnic there.
- Roll on the floor.
- Check out the thousand things you can do with a big cardboard box—always a winner with toddlers.
- Get in the bath with him and re-enact naval battles.

- Light candles and let him blow them out.
- Get all the pots out and make an orchestra with him.
- Look for insects and worms in the garden.
- Teach him to squirt water from his mouth in the garden, in the bath, at the beach.
- Introduce to him the wonder of ropes: he doesn't need to learn knots right now, but just getting ropes and tying each other up; loops; tugs of war—your toddler will love it.
- Take him on trains—any trains—going anywhere. Be prepared to take off your civilised persona and be really, really scared of the tunnels!

You'll notice none of those suggestions involved purchased toys! That's because although toys are great, they are not essential tools for play.

Our advice is to be really observant of your individual boy—note what makes him happy, sad, insecure, excited, angry or loving. Work out his drivers and where he sits on the testosterone hormonal spectrum—is he happiest with his shirt off mucking around in the dirt with his trucks or kicking a ball around outside, or does he love dressing up his dolls and asking his big sister to paint his fingernails? The important thing is that you provide a secure environment in which he can explore and learn at his own pace, in his own time and in his own way.

Observe who your baby boy is without judgement—the people he most needs acceptance and love from are his parents. And trust yourself—you'll know your boy better than anyone else. It's really important to know who he is—and who other boys are—and then ask yourself: 'What does my individual boy bring into the world?', 'What makes him happy and secure?' Then help co-create the environment he needs to thrive.

We encourage you to be strong about this; lots of well-meaning friends, family and complete strangers will offer you plenty of advice about what your boy should be doing, but you know your son best—be faithful to who he is becoming.

The really important thing is that children—particularly boys—are not shamed for being who they are. Kids are naturally adventurous and should have the freedom to explore all facets of being human. If they are shamed into being something or someone they are not, it often leads to depression in later life as they try to subjugate their true inner self. Don't walk down that road.

Finding his 'No!'

So the honeymoon is over and your cute one- to two-year-old little man starts pushing back. 'No!' is his favourite word and tantrums are frequent. They can happen anytime—anywhere—and no amount of placating, cajoling, threatening or bribery will snap him out of it. He'll throw himself on the floor, flailing his little limbs for all he's worth. 'Impulse control' is a foreign country to this wee man as he tries out everything from head banging to high-pitched screaming that'll rip your eardrums and fray your nerves to shreds. It's about now that parenting gets really interesting!

Being conscious of how you were disciplined (or not) matters a lot now because the likelihood is you'll revert to your early childhood parenting model—particularly when you're stressed by 'bad' behaviour. We're not talking about a pity-fest of self-indulgent navel-gazing—just a realistic look at how things went down for you in your childhood. Were you yelled at or whacked if you didn't do what you were told? Sent to your room? Sat on the naughty chair? Were you shamed if you stuffed up? What did that feel like?

It's time to talk to your partner about this now, so you both understand where you are coming from with boundary setting and discipline. In an ideal world, you will have discussed some aspects of parenting, including boundary setting and discipline, before your baby arrives. Don't assume you have similar ideas, as much of this is largely unconscious and will be flushed out—something that generally happens in situ, in the heat of the moment.

The conversation could go something like this: 'So I know smacking is illegal—what do you think are good alternatives?'; 'How do you feel about bribery, i.e. rewards for positive behaviour or removing them for negative behaviours?'; 'What sort of food should he be eating? The same as us?'; 'Should we make him finish all his food?'; 'What are your thoughts on hygiene? I think he should be able to get dirty as part of his development—do you?'; 'How do you feel about swearing?' (See 'He's got a potty mouth!' on page 27.)

We'll say here we don't agree with smacking. We rarely hit our kids—and the times we did, we sorely regretted it. There were other things we could and should have tried on those rare occasions. And now the science says that alternative, non-violent disciplines would have worked better. A recent report—*The Science of Corporal Punishment*—analysed four decades of research on smacking, and 88 studies involving 36,000 people 'were in agreement that while smacking may temporarily have corrected behavioural issues, it was not more productive than less violent forms of discipline'. The report's findings are chilling: 'Even if you spank with control, discipline, and good intent, your kids are more likely to have depression and engage in aggressive behaviour in adulthood.' Think very carefully about that.

As you have conversations with your partner, you will uncover your thoughts and expectations about behaviours and consequences and it will make parenting a whole lot easier. Because the truth is, most people come unstuck over these issues. If you don't have these conversations, you could find yourselves looking at each other aghast and wondering, 'Who is this irrational monster?'

It's important for parents to work together through this stage— don't play yourselves off against each other, because your boy will go for the gap if there is one. Sometimes your co-parent will set a boundary you don't agree with. Don't confront it in front of your child—let them follow it through (unless it's downright abusive!) and talk about it together later. Make a plan for how you'll handle that situation next time around.

If you're on your own it could be good to 'contract' a friend to buddy you through the hard patches. Someone you can have a rant to, reflect and strategise with—someone who'll remind you that your son's behaviour is not personal, he's just being a boy. Most of all, make sure the friend is someone you can laugh with. Because boy—are you ever gonna need your sense of humour!

Being consistent is key to great parenting—make boundaries clear and consistent, realistic but firm. Your boy will feel safe because he knows the rules and learns there will be a consistent response if he breaks them. Being firm without emotion is also important. We are not saying never show emotion; there will be times when what he's done—broken Grandma's special teacup; written on your newly painted walls—will make you bloody mad. You need to express that anger and your boy needs to see that, so he knows an adult can be angry and still remain in control—that his adult doesn't join him on Planet No Impulse Control!

But this is not the time to set the boundary or consequence. For one thing, all your boy will hear/see is your anger—not the words, and it will be too tempting to shame him.

Tell him you're really angry and need time to calm down. You'll get back to him about the consequence. Then remove either him or yourself from the situation and take some deep breaths . . .

It's really important to take a step back from these tough situations; draw a few deep breaths; put things in perspective and remember 'this too will pass'. Actually repeat those words as you take some deep breaths in . . . and out . . . in . . . and out . . . 'This too will pass.' It's amazing how deep breathing can help us regain control of ourselves.

When you feel a little calmer, try dropping down to his height and looking him in the eyes as you lower your voice and calmly set the boundary or consequence. Keep the language really simple and focused on what you want, without long explanations, so your toddler understands your words. And remember you are saying no to his specific behaviour, not to him generally: 'I don't like it when you . . .'; 'We don't do . . . in this family'; 'I'm taking your . . . until tomorrow because you didn't listen'.

Important: never ask your toddler for permission to set a boundary or consequence. For example, say, 'You hurt the cat—I'm taking your bear away'—not, 'I'm taking your bear away—OK?' or 'Do you understand if you do that again I'm going to have to take your bear away from you?' Do not walk down this road! Because remember: *you* are the adult and *you* set the boundaries at this stage.

Think of it as communicating via semaphore to another ship across an ocean—fewer, simpler words will get the message across. Later, as his rational brain begins kicking in more—by about four—you can begin to negotiate some.

Remember, what we're doing here is striving to be consistent—the reality is we will fail time and time again. The important thing is that you learn from your mistakes and get back on the horse. Overall it's the amount of consistency that matters—if you can be consistent two-thirds of the time you're doing bloody well! And this will have an impact on your boy.

He may also be pushing his physical boundaries by now—maybe trying to bite, punch or kick to see what reaction he gets. Don't ignore this—yes, we know it's really tempting to put this behaviour in the 'too hard' basket, but if ever there was a time to engage with your boy it is now. Deal directly with the conflict using words if you can, or simply hold him strongly as he flails around; take him outside; take him to his bedroom; or to his time-out or 'thinking' place/chair; and—as you look him directly in the eyes—keep talking in calm, measured words. If he doesn't calm down and needs time out on his own, calmly tell him you will come back soon. Keep going back until he has calmed down.

Then encourage him to 'use his words' if he's angry, and model this. Tell him the words/phrases he can use when he's annoyed or frustrated. 'I don't like it when you . . .'; 'You hurt my feelings'; 'I was playing with . . .'.

What we know is that this challenging, irrational behaviour seems to slowly phase out from about the age of four, if handled well. The tantrums are less ferocious and don't last as long. Some reasoning capacity has kicked in and the art of negotiation has some currency. That so many of us survive this stage is a miracle!

Be there

Engagement isn't just about the good times, folks—we're talking engagement in good times and bad; the interesting and downright boring times. We are all busy and it's easy to think 'I don't have time for this' and only half engage, but we say engage fully; be fully present to your boy, even if just for a few minutes at a time. Fill him up with your attention, then back off to let him find his own self-attention.

Engagement is about being real—being who you are; your authentic self—not putting on a 'parent voice' (you know, the one your non-parent friends use: 'Hello, Billy! Are you being a good boy for your daddy?'). It's being genuinely interested in what your boy is saying or doing. It's about suggesting play ideas: 'Let's play aeroplanes'; 'Want a shoulder ride?' It's about checking out his feelings: 'You look sad to me.' It's about reflecting back what you see or experienc: 'Man, you are so strong'; 'You helped tidy up really well.'

One thing that worries us is 'distracted parenting'—namely, parents in playgrounds flicking through social media or reading emails on their mobiles while their kids desperately plead for attention: 'Watch me climb this, Mum'; 'See how fast I can run, Dad.' Parent briefly looks up—'Yeah, that's great, son'—then back to the mobile.

Please consider dialling out of your electronic toys when you're with your boy unless the communication is really important—otherwise he's getting this distracted parent who isn't really engaged with him. The message you are giving him is that someone/something else is more important than him. A lot of the time. Really?

Maybe try telling your boss/workmate/acquaintance/friend-of-your-cousin's-half-sister-twice-removed that you're busy right now playing with your son—you'll call/text them back later. Because it's him who is most likely to be around for the rest of your life, and the more energy you pour into him in these early years, the more likely it is he'll hang around and be there for you in your grey, wrinkly, forgetful stage (unlike the aforementioned people).

He's got a potty mouth!

Kids love saying rude words. Bum, poo, bugger, shit, fuck . . . you'll hear them all from the time your boy learns to talk. We never said anything much to our kids about swearing—mainly for fear of gross hypocrisy! And given that American research confirms nearly two-thirds of adults with rules about their children swearing found they regularly broke their own rules, we think we were on the right track not making a big deal out of it.

Dr Timothy Jay, a psychologist and expert in swearing (is this really a job?!), reckons our efforts to keep language clean are probably futile. He discovered that by the age of six, children have a pretty broad vocabulary of swear words and that boys swear more than girls—quite a lot more. So that's something to look forward to.

We think Dr Jay's right. We can report that none of our kids, as adults, have bad potty mouths, despite the lack of discipline around swearing, so we must have done something right. We figured they'd learn the hard way, which they did. Once, daughter number two chanced her luck by saying 'fuck' at her nana's place—something she only did once, after hell's fury rained down on her tiny head! It's good to remember that most kids are agile survivors, well capable of moderating their behaviour appropriate to the conditions.

When our kids went through a particularly bad swearing patch we decided to give them five minutes' swear time a day; they could say anything they liked for five minutes then the rest of the day was swear-free. Man did they go for it during those five minutes! Every time the swear time ended in uproarious laughter.

On reflection, what we were teaching them was there is a time for swearing and a time for not swearing—simple. Once, our son, exasperated at his sisters' teasing, yelled at the top of his voice, 'You fuckeeeeerrrrrrrs!' Everyone stopped—there was a deep silence—we were all pretty shocked by his outburst. But the outcome was his sisters backed off and he gained some mana. It's become a family story now and some of us are known, when exasperated by certain situations, to repeat his outburst!

Swearing is one of those things you either decide to make an issue of or you don't—to us they were just words and we figured, given all the challenges a blended family throws at you, that we had much bigger fish to fry.

Igniting his imagination

Albert Einstein said imagination is more important than knowledge. We agree. When you think about it, most of what is important and useful to the world started off as an idea in someone's head—in their imagination. Like any other human capacity, imagination can be grown by giving it the light of our attention—empowering it with our enthusiasm—or it can wither and decline through lack of use or respect.

Imagination is mostly developed through play. Men also start building their sense of morality in their boyhood, mainly through their own imaginative play and their play with other boys. They may clash crudely in play over basic moral actions like stealing or sharing, but they will later imagine their way through the finer detail of those actions and understand how they could do it differently next time. We learn from our mistakes through imagination; imagining how it could have been had we acted differently. Mistakes can be great teachers but only if we have the humility to accept we erred and the imagination to change.

The development of a man's imagination starts in boyhood with imaginative play, where the boy is literally playing with his imagination. As he's digging tunnels through mounds of dirt he's imagining a new universe at the end of those tunnels; as he's running on the beach he's imagining standing on the podium accepting his medal . . .

Imagination has two homes: the singular, inside your boy's head, and the collective, when he engages in play with other children or you. Singular imagination can come out best in unstructured play—that is, when your boy is exploring himself and engaging with his environment. Structured games and single-purpose toys are fine and do much to help develop your boy's motor skills but they don't always require his imagination. Building, drawing, painting, mucking around with ropes and anything to do with water are the fertile grounds for imagination as your boy turns visual, tactile experiences into inner stories and mythic images.

Stories are another doorway into imagination, especially if they are told by you with just the minimum of pictures, if any. A told story requires your boy to create the world and characters of the story in his head—a capacity he will need when he learns to read later. That capacity will feed him for the rest of his life.

Collective imagination is quite different. Just watch and listen to some children as they negotiate play. Someone comes up with an idea; others build on it or destroy it for something better. Your boy's imagination is getting a social work-out and he is learning crucial lessons about collaborating with others, about accepting other's imaginary words and worlds, about how others can help build his ideas into something bigger, better or just outright more beautiful than he could ever have imagined on his own.

We think imagination is one of the roots of empathy; to see yourself in someone else's shoes you need to imagine yourself as another person. The better you can do that, the more likely you will be to develop empathy; the better your imagination, the more nuanced your empathy will be.

Our morals and ethics may be inherited from family and culture but we need an active imagination to give these morals life in our souls. We have to imagine what 'good' or 'bad' looks like in any given situation; we need to think through the options and alternatives of our actions in a moral sense, and while some of this may be rational thinking, we will need imagination to really embrace the nuances of moral behaviour. It teaches us the difference between obeying the cultural rules of human interaction and knowing the right behaviour in any situation.

Our experience is you can't force boys to be interested in anything—you can just offer stuff and watch to see if it ignites their imagination. Don't censor his imaginary, creative world; if he wants to play with dolls, let him—it's not really any different from playing with toy soldiers. And remember, when he's playing with dolls, he's learning about empathy in the same way girls do, and why not? We all want our men to grow up to be aware of and empathic towards others. He may want to try wearing dresses and nail polish—maybe even try out some make-up (especially true if he's got an older sister with an interest in these things). Let him do it. And don't worry about the implications for his sexuality; play choices in childhood are not necessarily an indicator of sexual preference—that's something he'll sort out for himself later.

It does start to get trickier once boys spend more time in the social sphere—i.e. day-care or school, where if they play with dolls they are likely to be shamed. However, you have to roll with it—our very strong-willed, three-year-old grandson insisted on wearing his beloved pink skirt to day-care and wore it all day, despite one of the teachers reporting they'd called him the girls' derivative of his name all day. Obviously some holes in the ECE training curriculum!

And don't worry if your boy has imaginary friends. Research tells us that by the age of seven, some 37 per cent of kids have them; they either appear alone or in groups. Interestingly, boys tend to invent only male imaginary friends, whereas girls have either male or female ones. Oldest and only children, and children who don't watch much television are more likely to have an imaginary friend, probably because children need unstructured time alone to be able to invent imaginary friends.

If imaginary friends arrive into your boy's life, we say welcome them—they can be helpful allies and will have no effect on his mental health. We don't think it's wise to be intrusive by wanting to know too much about your boy's imaginary friends, or even refer to them too much; they are, after all, not your imaginary friends (hey, get your own!). They are your boy's way of relating to himself and making sense of his world.

So he's a bit bored

We've established that men need a rich, healthy inner world—the ability to think and imagine, to remember and synthesise—if they are to form their own moral compass and sense of character. That inner world starts in boyhood, often through the gateway of boredom.

As parents, we seem to be scared of boredom, tripping over ourselves to fill this apparent vacuum with activity and stimulus. But boredom is a great teacher of self-motivation and the importance of imagination in forming character. We say, when your boy shows or complains of boredom, don't immediately rush in—let it be; let your boy wallow in boredom for a while until his imagination kicks in and he starts scratching around in the dirt, tinkering pointlessly as something emerges, or simply picks himself up off the couch and walks out to the great outdoors. Give boredom a little time.

Your boy is now learning the basics of self-motivation, self-teaching, self-stimulation. He is learning he cannot rely on the outside world and you, in particular, to stimulate him all the time. He's learning that his imagination is quite possibly the best ally he will ever have. Remember, one of the underlying causes of ADHD is the inability to self-stimulate, but more on that later (see page 91).

Discovering his willie

Your boy might also get interested in playing with his willie from about the age of one onwards. He'll get erections and hey, who isn't interested in the feelings that generates!

Many years ago, when I (Ruth) visited a tiny island off Tahiti, a group of us started playing with a frisbee, which the local kids had never seen before. To my then 18-year-old self's embarrassment, the little boys were so excited they sprung erections and started playing with themselves. I didn't know which way to look! But what it illustrated was that we overlay our primal sexuality with cultural mores, and that maybe we need to think about how stringently we want to enforce those mores.

Our advice is not to tell him off when he plays with himself—you'll only succeed in making him feel guilt and shame, and we all know what that does to the human psyche. If there's anything we've learned from interviewing over 650 men, it's don't shame them as boys—particularly around their sexuality—as that'll turn bad later.

However, you might want to explain that even though playing with yourself feels good, it might be best done in private; even pre-schoolers are old enough to understand that some things are simply not meant to be public. They're also old enough to understand that no one—not even family members or other people they trust—should ever touch them in a way that feels uncomfortable.

Kids will also start to play 'doctors' and 'boyfriends' and 'girlfriends' as they explore their sexuality. No need to panic, in our experience, as long as there is no age or power imbalance—but definitely step in if you see that happening. And of course you would dissuade them from actually trying to have sex—which we had to do once! If that's happening, it's probably time to bring out the junior anatomy books and start channelling their interest in the body into education about it. (See 'Let's talk about sex' on page 129 and 'He's doing it' on page 170 for more on sex for older boys.)

Bumps and bruises

Your boy is going to take plenty of tumbles on his road to manhood—of that you can be sure. So he needs to learn how to take risks experientially—that is, he needs to take risks and learn from the consequences of them. If he runs too fast he falls over; if he drops something heavy on his foot it hurts; if he punches someone or something he'll cause injury; if he cuts himself it hurts and blood comes out (which is quite impressive, really).

Of course we all want to keep our kids safe—shield them from pain—and we are not saying you should abandon all your protective instincts. But those instincts came about from your early experiences of bumps and tumbles and the pain that came with them, and your boy needs the same education you received. The point is to allow a reasonable level of risk-taking, knowing there will occasionally be cuts, scrapes and bruises—even a few broken bones and some stitches— but also knowing the lessons from these injuries will be invaluable for your boy's future.

Encouraging him to take risks early will save you both a great deal of anguish later. Look at it as money in the bank: the more he's learned about risk as a young fella, the less likely he is to find out about life-threatening risk when he's a teenager in charge of a motor-bike or car, or trying out adventure sports with new friends on foreign soil during his OE. That's the call you don't want to get.

Ours came at 5am one morning, saying there had been an avalanche in northern Japan, where our adult son was snowboarding with mates. News reports said four Kiwis were missing, presumed dead. No names would be released until relatives had been informed. Our world fell apart as we struggled to find out if our son, who we couldn't contact, was among them. We were close to hysterical.

We eventually convinced a radio reporter who had the names but couldn't release them to say 'Yes' or 'No' when we said our son's name. When she said 'No' we sobbed like babies. Our boy eventu-ally phoned, knowing we'd be worried. He said he knew those who had died, who were 'free boarders', snowboarding off the main routes. 'I'd never risk going out in back country like that,' he told us.

However, we agonised for the parents of the boys who lost their lives that day. How they coped with their grief we'll never know. But what we do know is that fear of our children dying or being maimed through experiencing the world is not a good reason to try to stop them doing it. All we can do is teach them about risk and hope enough information sinks in for them to make good decisions for themselves when they are faced with potentially dangerous situations in the future.

It's great to see some schools relaxing playground rules and encouraging adrenalin-enhancing games like bullrush (also known as kingasini), which was banned in many schools in the mid-1980s for fear of kids hurting themselves. Kids are learning so much as they navigate the gauntlet of ever-increasing taggers in bullrush, including strategy, physical and mental agility and teamwork, as the runners cooperate to outsmart the taggers. It's all good.

Also great to see kids' playgrounds now being designed with kids in mind—a novel approach! One brilliant example overseas is the nature playground at Valbyparken on the outskirts of Copenhagen, where there is no 'play equipment'—just low hills dotted with paths and walking tracks; a village of willow houses surrounded by wattle fences; areas with wild flowers and sand; a snail-shaped earthwork leading to a lookout point; climbing areas with ropes, etc. The entire area is enclosed by a footbridge, connecting five towers. There is also a cool fire pit and no shortage of mud when it rains. Stock up on laundry detergent, folks, because playing in mud is back!

Fortunately, there are a growing number of New Zealand companies also creating natural playground spaces—sometimes called 'outdoor living classrooms'—in parks, day-cares and schools, using materials like logs, stones, ropes and shells to ignite kids' imaginations. Sometimes they incorporate edible gardens that kids help to grow and can forage from. This is all really good news for our boys!

It's also important your boy learns where his limits are around his physical strength through activities like play-fighting. This is often seen as a father's domain but mums may find it really fun as well. Maybe you might need to invest in some breast plates, though! When you get down on the floor and tussle with your son, it's helping to educate him about cause and effect—what happens to another person when he punches or kicks them? How do they react? How strong is he? And he's learning about trust—can he trust you not to hurt him? How do you manage your impulses when he hits you too hard? This is big learning for your boy and best done when he's young and hasn't been subjected to 'virtual' fighting yet.

The reality is we live in a world filled with 'pretend fighting' in video games and movies, where the consequences are never really felt. We fool ourselves if we think play-fighting in an animated game or movie is safer than real play-fighting. It's one thing for your video opponent to be knocked to the ground but a whole other thing when you—through over-enthusiasm—knock your friend to the ground or the other way round, with the resulting pain, real blood and tears.

Making child-care decisions

This is a biggie. If you decide to send your boy to day-care (which we think should be renamed 'play-care'), either through choice or necessity, we think these two key questions will help guide you: 'Who is my boy?' and 'What sort of environment does he thrive in?'

Every boy is different—lots of them love being outdoors, running free and exploring natural environments, while some will be happy sitting in a corner with a book or doing other indoor activities.

However, our experience is that boys do better in day-care environments that are boy-friendly—where there are lots of outdoor spaces for them to explore and be loud in. Places where there are big sandpits they can turn into quarries; trees they can climb; trains they can watch going by; playhouses they can turn into forts; grass they can run on—the more running spaces the better!

It's great to see innovative—particularly boy-friendly—play-spaces being developed overseas, like the Fuji Kindergarten outside Tokyo (Google the TED talk 'The best kindergarten you've ever seen'). This building has a huge oval top storey that kids can circumnavigate at speed, and slides and ladders that descend to classrooms on the bottom level that have trees growing through them. We want to go to this kindy! Designers Takaharu and Yui Tezuka of Tezuka Architects credit their children for the kindergarten. 'All I had to do was think like a kid,' Takaharu Tezuka says in the TED talk. 'They became part of my body and as they grew up, their habits and desires became mine, and in designing the school with my wife, I only needed to channel them to know what to build.'

Fortunately, there are some great examples in New Zealand as well, like the Otaki Kindergarten where free-range kids fossick in gardens and dirt and build castles out of recycled plastic cartons and junk. There's lots of our beloved ropes and water and getting dirty is encouraged. Build them and the children will come!

So, if your boy falls into the active category, make sure you choose a day-care that he's going to thrive in. Our grandson is a very busy boy and despite there being a day-care attached to the university where our daughter works, she chose one much further away because of the superior outdoor spaces she knew her son would love. It's not always about convenience—it's about finding the right place for your boy.

If you find a centre with some male teachers, all the better! Currently only approximately 2 per cent of early childhood education teachers in New Zealand are male—but the numbers are growing, says education lecturer Alex Williams in a 2013 Unitec magazine article. The lack of men isn't solely due to fears about accusations of child abuse—which is statistically much more likely to happen in the home, by someone a child knows and trusts—nor about low pay rates, given that men often do other low-paid work; it's about societal attitudes to gender, says Williams. 'Society just doesn't see working with young children as something that men do. It's been framed up as a woman's activity, an extension of mothering, a nurturing and caring role and that's something we don't see as synonymous with what men do. This needs to change.'

Another option if you are returning to work, need time out from your toddler or think they would benefit from more stimulation is to look to your whanau. We looked after our grandchildren one day a week when they were little and there's something really special about this relationship, if it works for you all. Or, if your budget and living space allows for it, you can find a nanny or au pair. We are encouraged by the recent rise in the number of 'mannies'—male foreign students looking after Kiwi kids. Some friends had a French mannie who their son adored—he was a big outdoorsy guy who stretched their son with adventures as well as caring for him well.

There is some debate over whether young kids should be in day-care at all. Psychologist Steve Biddulph—author of *Raising Boys*—recommends that boys be looked after at home until the age of three. He theorises that boys in day-care are more likely to misbehave, particularly by being aggressive and disobedient; are more prone to anxiety that may harm development; and that day-care weakens the child's relationship with their parents, leaving the child prone to being emotionally shutdown.

But a study by the National Institute of Child Health and Human Development (NICHD) in the United States, which looked at the influence of both child care and the home environment on over 1000 typically developing children, found: 'Children who attend child care have the same outcomes as children who are cared for at home. Whether a child attends day-care or not, it is the family that has a major impact on their child's development, with the parents' interactions with the child being a critically important factor.'

The two family features that had the most significant influence on children's development were the quality of mother-child interactions—children's outcomes were better when mothers were responsive, sensitive, attentive and provided good stimulation during interactions—and the family environment. Unsurprisingly, families which had organised routines, access to books and play materials, and engaged in stimulating experiences both in and out of the home (outings, library trips, etc.) had children with better social and cognitive outcomes.

The NICHD study also found that, compared to a control group in other types of care, centre-based child care was linked to:

- somewhat better cognitive and language development
- better pre-academic skills involving letters and numbers
- fewer behaviour problems at ages two and three
- greater behaviour problems at age four and a half (such as disobedience and aggression).

There are countless arguments for and against day-care. In the end we believe each family has to make an individual decision based on their circumstances and their particular boy.

If you go down the day-care route, there are bound to be some tears initially—on both sides. The reality is, there will always be a bit of pain at the gate but the important thing to find out is does he settle when you're not there? Take him along to a few day-cares for a test session —you'll get a pretty good steer on where he's happiest, which could be at home.

Despite our best efforts, we had to abandon day-care in favour of home-based care for our youngest daughter, who never settled in day-care. She simply couldn't tolerate the level of stimulation, which manifested as hysterical behaviour, and in the end we accepted it wasn't for her.

Here are few things to weigh up:

- Who is my boy?
- What does he enjoy doing?
- How does he interact with other kids?
- How does he respond to other adults, particularly when you're not there?
- How many male early childhood education teachers are working at the centre? (When you visit, watch to see if and how they do things differently to female teachers.)
- What is the centre's attitude towards play—are they a managed-risk or a cotton-wooling centre?
- What is the balance between cognitive learning and play? (Err on the side of more play.)
- Is home-based care an option?

- Is day-care beneficial for both your boy and his caregivers (often the mum but increasingly a combo of mum and dad and/or extended family)?
- What can you afford?

He's a quirky kid

Some kids are just more different than others. They're quirky and march to the beat of their own drum. When all the other kids are happily playing together they're off on their own doing whatever activity is currently engrossing them. Disturb them at your peril! They may have sensory sensitivity—they don't like the way tags feel in clothes or don't like particular fibres such as wool. Maybe they don't like loud noises, or bright lights, or people wearing heavy make-up or costumes.

Quirky kids can be hard to consequence and sometimes hard to love because of their challenging behaviours. Everyone from well-meaning relatives to acquaintances will offer up their sage advice on what you should do about your oddball kid. 'You're not firm enough with him', 'You should set tougher boundaries', 'You mollycoddle him too much', 'You're making a rod for your own back'. 'Wow—if only I'd thought of that!' you'll think sarcastically to yourself as you smile and quietly remove your weirdo kid from public view!

Parents often end up agonising over their quirky kids—wondering if they are just unusual or on a spectrum of some sort, which has much greater implications for their futures. It really all depends on the level of intensity of their particular quirkiness, whether they are out of the normative category and into the pathological area, and whether it gets in the way of their socialisation and/or learning.

In our case it did. Having raised three relatively 'normal' children, our youngest daughter didn't meet any of the normal developmental milestones, had unusual behaviours and wasn't having a bar of our discipline. At age five she soundly put us in our place when she announced: 'You can't tell me what to do! You're here to look after me but I'm the boss of myself!' Well, that was us told! Needless to say her development and education had an unusual and challenging trajectory that required significant input from both us and her educators, but she has recently graduated as a social worker and we are very proud of her. Her quirkiness is evening out over time and will be her gift to the world.

Dr Mark Bowers, clinical director at Brighton Center for Paediatric Neurodevelopment in Michigan, United States, and author of *8 Keys to Raising the Quirky Child: How to Help a Child Who Doesn't (Quite) Fit In*, said in a Radio New Zealand National interview that the defining questions when you've got a quirky kid are: 'Is this a problem or not?' and 'Is their "quirk" just their style or is it interfering with their socialisation?'

'A quirky child experiences difficulty fitting in and connecting with others, usually due to an interpersonal style or behaviour that stands out from the other kids. Maybe they are obsessed with a topic of interest or spend excessive hours a day reading or playing with just one toy. These kids are not so far afield as to fall on the autism spectrum, but they are unique, and their behaviours are not addressed in typical parenting books,' Dr Bowers said.

The key, said Dr Bowers, is to catch quirkiness young, so you can help your kid. His book is full of tips and strategies for parents of kids who are 'different'. For example, if your boy is socially awkward—misqueuing or reading social situations wrongly—parents can help by setting up appropriate play dates and staying involved in the play.

Quirky kids need mediation and coaching to learn socialisation, so get involved early if you sense your boy is different—more support early will give him the best possible shot at being happy and reaching his potential later—and let's face it, that's all any of us want.

If you feel your son is more than quirky, you'll need expert involvement in diagnosing, treating and managing his condition. The best place to start is a conversation with your doctor.

Summary

Congratulations on surviving the first four years! So far we've established:

- Your son will learn from who you are rather than from what you tell him.
- He's having testosterone surges that will affect his growth and behaviour.
- His brain isn't physically fully formed until he's about three.
- Mum's the word at this early stage but fathers are really important.
- Dad should be at the birth if possible and bond with his boy as early as he can.
- Bonding—'attachment'—is critical to healthy growth.
- This stage is all about play, play, play.
- Be fully present when you are with your son—tune out from your devices.
- Your boy has likely found his 'no' and may start swearing.

- There are better ways of disciplining than smacking.
- He's also discovered his willie!
- You're igniting his imagination through play . . .
- . . . but also letting him be bored sometimes, because boredom is the doorway to imagination.
- You've started implementing consistent boundaries and consequences.
- You're slowly encouraging your son to use his words rather than his fists.
- Through things like play-fighting you begin encouraging him to take risks.
- He may be covered in plasters and bruise cream.
- You've made some decisions about child care.
- You've worked out if he's a bit quirky, and how to start dealing with it.

The most important of these is, we believe, that your boy soaks up and learns from who you are, rather than from what you tell him—about either yourself or how the world works. His world view is being shaped by watching everything you do and what he sees and experiences will, in turn, shape who he becomes. Aspiring to be the best person you can imagine will be the singular biggest gift you give your boy as he heads out on the road to manhood.

TWO

Stepping out: 4 to 7 years

My favourite colour is red because it's the only fast colour—all the other colours are too slow.

Charlie (4 years)

You've navigated the toddler tantrums and your baby is starting to look like a big boy—there might even be times when you glimpse the man he will become; his archetype. Is he soft, caring, determined, intelligent, physical, dextrous, satisfied, happy, melancholic, serious, aggressive, bolshie, a go-getter or placid? Try to notice who he is becoming. It will give you a good steer on what he needs from you. Hopefully he's reasonably well attached to you and is happily exploring his expanding environment. Because the good news here is that it's still playtime!

Your son's cognitive abilities are increasing as his frontal cortex slowly controls more of his learning—a process that will be substantially complete by about the age of seven, after which he effectively learns the same way you do.

Until then, what he still needs to be learning are social and emotional skills, rather than cognitive ones, so that's where your focus needs to be. If you're opening up play opportunities for him, helping him learn to use his words instead of his feet or fists, teaching him to negotiate over toys and games, encouraging him to control his impulses, and increasing his resilience through play and managed risk-taking, go to the top of the class, you good parent!

Your boy may or may not have a testosterone surge at about the age of four—the jury is still out on this, with English psychologist and author of parenting and child-care books Sarah Ockwell-Smith saying on her website there is no evidence for it and challenging us to stop blaming the failings of modern society on a hormone. She writes that behavioural problems associated with boys in this age group lie with 'Us, me, you, parents, adults, society . . . Little boys (and that is what a four year old is) need to play, play, play, play, play and play some more. They need open space, nature, air. They need trees to climb, balls to kick, mud to squelch, Frisbees to throw. They need to be allowed to use their amazing imaginations and explore the world with their whole bodies.'

Ockwell-Smith says what boys get instead are school, schedules, strict rules, being told to sit still, getting cooped up inside, told not to speak unless they raise their hand—and screen time. 'These things and four year old boys don't mix,' she writes. The outcome is a lot of frustration that either gets internalised by the child and manifests as anxiety, depression or withdrawal, or externalised via punching, kicking, hitting, etc.

So to be really clear about this, we are saying hold back on intellectual or cognitive efforts with your son until he's over five. We know this goes against what you'll hear from early childhood educationalists and educationalists generally, particularly in New Zealand, where there is a focused drive towards early childhood learning. There will be some pressure from others to get your boy engaged in early reading or numeracy work, based on the idea that the earlier kids start, the better they'll do later. We are clearly saying that early intellectual work does *not* help later and may in fact cause problems for your son down the track. (See 'Hothousing is bollocks' on page 83.) We prefer to think of this stage as the time for laying solid *foundations* for mental and intellectual development. That solid ground is the social, emotional and creative worlds developed in play and through the most powerful creative force we humans have, the imagination.

Your boy may begin moving away from his mother a little by now, as he begins to experience himself as separate from her, and, assuming his father is around, may start to notice him more. This is the time for fathers to say, 'Hello, I'm one of you—welcome to the man tribe' and begin to do a lot more with their sons.

The best advice we can give to fathers at this stage is to be the man you want your son to become. How you operate as a man in the world really matters, because maleness is caught—not taught. He's watching your every move—the way you talk; relate to women (particularly his mum); talk to other men; how clothes hang on you; how you talk about your work; what you drink, eat, read and watch. His brain cells are in overdrive figuring out what kind of man you are so he can begin his human task of becoming his own man.

We're talking about emotional intelligence here, men—the ability to reflect on your life and be mindful of how you relate to others is critical to your modelling 'good man' to your son. If you know yourself and your emotional drivers, you can stand strongly in the world. Your boy will sort of just nudge up against you and come along for the male ride.

Pressure off, dads—the good news is you don't have to be a perfect male role model. You simply have to be authentic and self-aware. Your son is smart enough to not only observe how you operate in the world, but also to notice how you reflect on what you do and how you act. For example, say your son sees you pump your ego in front of your mates to impress them. A bit later you could 'allow' him to hear you 'thinking aloud' about how silly that was. Or say you've yelled at your boy and shamed him in some way. You come back and apologise to him—not for telling him off, but for shaming him. He is soaking up that maleness can be reflective and mindful, flawed but redeemable.

There's no shortage of jokes about men being emotional Neanderthals—incapable of reflecting on their last meal, let alone their motivations—but our experience of matching many hundreds of men to be mentors to fatherless boys is that they enjoy the invitation to reflect on their lives. Many, many times, when we ask them to consider their own childhoods as part of mentor training, they'll say, 'Wow, I've never thought about this before.' It may be new to them but they 'get it' and they're away; it can be the beginning of a journey as they realise they can either keep stumbling through life or have as their leading question, 'What was it like for me as a boy?'

That's the wonderful gift of parenting—it will develop you in ways you could never have imagined. You were probably thinking it's you teaching him to be a man—well, you are . . . but he's teaching you as well. Put bluntly, being a father will make a man out of you.

Mums on their own can start to look to grandfathers, uncles and friends for a man to whom their boy responds and really encourage that relationship. Remember, at Big Buddy, we deal with a very small proportion—probably 10 to 20 per cent—of solo-mother households where there are no adult males around. That means 80 to 90 per cent of solo-mother households *do* have access to a mentor for their boys, and for a large number, that's their father. But if he's not around or is unsafe, it's now time to find that good man to be a model for your boy. (See 'Father hunger' on page 50.)

Ultimately, growing great boys is all about mana—it's all about your presence, about your confidence in who you are, regardless of your sex. We all remember the teacher who walked into class and the students were immediately quiet. They just have some presence that says 'I'm in charge here' and boys, especially, really respect that—up until a certain age, where they'll start to test the boundaries!

A word of warning, though—boys have really well-developed bullshit detectors that can sense who people really are. So there is no point in pretending. You cannot fake this stuff; it's more important to be honestly who you are, warts and all, than to be perfect. Having their instincts confirmed by you being authentic builds a strong image of maleness in boys—it teaches them to trust their hunches.

It's an anchor point they are looking for, not a blueprint. They will grow and develop their own unique expression of maleness, but the seeds for that come from those authentic parts of you they soaked up and absorbed as boys.

If you try to be someone or something you are not, it is just plain confusing to them and will lead boys off their path. (See 'Ancestor worship' on page 67.)

Father hunger

Father hunger starts really kicking in for boys at around six to seven. Ask any male teacher and he'll tell you that's when he starts to notice the fatherless boys—the needy ones who hang out for his attention when the others are off playing. It's why we accept fatherless boys onto the Big Buddy programme at seven. By that age we know they have moved away from their mums enough to feel secure with an adult male who they don't know. Up until then they simply aren't ready for the separation from Mum.

Psychologist and author Steve Biddulph says in *Raising Boys* that there is a 'switching on' of boys' masculinity at this age. 'Even boys who have not watched any TV suddenly want to play with swords, wear Superman capes, fight and wrestle, and make lots of noise.'

At about six, says Steve Biddulph, 'Boys will "lock on" to their dads, stepdads or whichever male is around, and want to be with him, learn from him and copy him. They want to "study how to be a male".'

There's a hierarchy of ideal men but the truth is that most boys want their father, regardless of what their mother thinks of him. This is particularly true if he was around when the boy was born. They just know he's 'the guy'. If he's disappeared from the boy's life for whatever reason, then mothers can help them find another guy to attach to and as soon as they attach to that man, he becomes 'the guy'. (At Big Buddy we've proved that once a boy attaches to his mentor, he's 'the man'.) The bottom line is, boys need contact with adult men and whoever you can find is good, as long as he's a safe, good-hearted man.

We use the words 'good-hearted' deliberately; he does not have to be perfect, he does not have to be the ideal male archetype. He simply has to be a man capable of kindness and humour who is comfortable in his own skin; someone you'd like to have as your own uncle or brother.

The first place to look for your boy's man is within your wider family/whanau—brothers, uncles, grandfathers, etc. Those men will, of course, have some kind of interest in your son but that may change when you say, 'My son needs a father figure in his life—can that be you?' It may not have occurred to your brother, uncle or father to step up but when you ask, it does two things: firstly, it tells him there's a job to be done here (men generally get that), and secondly, that you trust him to be that father figure. He may not have thought of himself in that way until you asked.

You don't need to restrict your boy's man to one man though—we reckon the more father figures the better! Your boy will be more than capable of male bonding with more than one guy. With someone from outside of your family, it may feel trickier; how do you know he's going to be safe, good-hearted and a worthy father figure? At this age, it's simply enough that your son meets and experiences adult men— later he will need more and we'll explore that. (See 'Safety around other men' on page 123.)

If you're 'the man', it's time to start doing lots of stuff with your boy—remember, you won't always share the same interests but give as many activities as you can a shot and see if they fly. Some things he'll like—others you will. By checking out lots of different activities you'll slowly sort out common interests and can creatively expand on them. At this age boys are generally happy to go along with whatever you suggest, so go for it—we're talking blue-sky thinking here. (See 'Activity suggestions for younger boys' on page 102.)

Trust what feels right and don't think you have to steer activities towards 'blokey stuff'—your boy is picking up maleness not so much by what you do, but by how you do it. The main thing your boy will learn is about learning; about having confidence in curiosity and turning it into action. When you say, 'I have no idea how to build a catapult but I reckon we can learn how to make one,' and then do it, he's learning he can give things a go—and that's the most important learning of all. Remember, if you don't know how to do or make something, Google it—you can just about guarantee YouTube will have it covered. If they haven't, post your own video once you've sussed it—your boy will love that!

Lookee me, Mum!

Our advice to mothers at this stage is to stay loving towards and connected with your son but learn to step back some—give him more rope. Be part of encouraging your boy to get outside and explore his world. Help him expand it. Really examine your fears about the world before you limit your son's exploration of it. Don't be the fun police—overreacting if he gets dirty, climbs too high, runs too fast or learns to cut with a knife. Let him get dirty; just make sure he's got plenty of play clothes (think *The Sound of Music* tree-climbing clothes instead of expensive designer ones—save those for visits to the rellies). You shouldn't tape him down because of your fears or anxieties. Remember, the more he learns about taking managed risks at an early age, the fewer big risks he'll take as a teenager. We reckon it's better to be part of that risk education early, so your boy trusts you when he really needs advice later.

The basic message for mothers here is 'don't overreact'; don't pour too much emotion into your reactions. If Dad or someone else is doing something with your boy that makes you scared, stand back, take a deep breath and examine the situation before you react. If the danger is really just in your head and he's unlikely to be badly hurt, walk away and let him take the risk. If it is truly dangerous, sure you should step in, but try to set a boundary without too much emotion. Don't transfer your fear to him because all he'll get is 'Jeeez . . . Mum's really scared, Mum's really scared'—and he'll focus on making it right for you instead of learning anything about the potential risk he was about to take.

In *The Male Brain,* American doctor Louann Brizendine says research shows the particular way dads play with their children makes their kids more curious and improves their ability to learn. 'Dad play' is more stimulating because it's more creative and unpredictable. Dads will change out songs and stories, whereas mothers tend to stick to the text.

A German study that followed kids for 15 years found that the ones whose fathers played roughly with them were the most self-confident when they hit adolescence. Men also tease their kids more and do the crazy role-playing thing that can drive mums mad—along with the 'poo-bum-fart' banter! But according to researchers, this kind of father-child play improves a kid's ability to guess what's on another person's mind and to recognise tricks and deceits. That's got to be good. All the foolishness that makes mums wonder if they've got an extra big kid on their hands in the form of their partner is actually an excellent contribution to growing a great boy.

There's a lot of debate about how children transition from childhood to becoming good citizens of the world, but everyone agrees it does involve some risk-taking. In Japan, for example, children as young as two are sent out on errands and as young as six catch trains and buses on their own. Unthinkable to us! But Dr Dwayne Dixon, a cultural anthropologist from Duke University in North Carolina, told

Radio New Zealand National it's a common sight, particularly in rural areas, where parents are familiar and comfortable with their neighbourhoods.

'The parents want to encourage their children to trust neighbours and shopkeepers—to teach their children trust. They are teaching them not so much independence, as dependence on a number of trustworthy adults,' said Dr Dixon.

Dr Dixon said this helps engender a sense of belonging to their communities. If the child gets into trouble, they know someone they trust will help them. This sense of shared responsibility across the community is a training ground for incorporating children into wider society.

We're not suggesting you send your two-year-old son on an errand or put your six-year-old on a bus, but maybe we all need to think more about how we build resilience in kids, through encouraging them to take more managed risks instead of cotton-wooling them—particularly boys—and setting up 'panic sites' around them where everything they do is wrong or potentially dangerous. Giving kids the message that the world is an unsafe place with danger lurking round every corner is not going to help them and ultimately, we shoot ourselves in the foot because they're too damned scared to ever leave home! Not the result we're looking for, people.

So if, for example, your boy is climbing a tree and grabs a thin branch that breaks and he falls, spraining his ankle, and an adult who he knows helps your son limp home—don't overreact! Your boy has learned two invaluable lessons:

1. Don't trust thin branches! Carefully gauge risk and limits of support before you put your faith in them. Be smart about reaching beyond your experience.

2. Others will be there to help, i.e. we all need help from others at times, so fostering relationships is a good thing. Bugger that man alone/hero stereotype—give things your best shot but reach out for help when you need it.

The gift of self-reflection

Self-reflection (or at least an attempt at it) is the number-one parenting tool in our book. As your son participates more in the world, more and more questions and challenges are going to be raised for you, requiring deeper self-reflection, as you head into the land-mine country of making decisions about everything from what clothes he wears to schooling and religious instruction.

Mums may become more fearful about safety, and there could be argy-bargy between the parents over what Dad is doing with his boy and what Mum thinks is safe. The challenges that come up now might be around:

- **How's he dressed?** Dads often have a much looser approach to clothing than mums, who worry about warmth in winter in an effort to ward off colds and flus. Sometimes clothes have to be glaringly ill-fitting before Dad will notice, whereas Mum is already planning next season's wardrobe. We used to joke that our son's undies would have to be cutting off the circulation in his legs before his dad would notice he needed new ones! So it's good to talk about clothing and try to reach a consensus on what's appropriate for outside play in winter, social occasions, etc. Talk about what causes illness and what the real risks are.

- **How should we discipline him?** The root cause of many
  a parental spat! As we've said, if you haven't reflected on
  how you were disciplined as a kid, you will likely default to
  disciplining your kids the way you were disciplined. This
  approach may cause friction if your partner questions your
  methods. 'Too harsh,' say the mothers. 'Too soft,' say the
  dads. Research shows that dads do dole out harsher discipline
  than mothers, so chances are you'll have differing views on
  the why, when and how much of discipline. Talk through
  how you feel about him talking back; swearing; hitting;
  not doing jobs; stealing; ignoring instructions, etc. What
  consequences should there be? (See 'Boundary setting' on
  page 78.)

- **Which school should he go to?** Your boy is about to spend
  six hours a day with his peers, soaking up their collective
  wisdom. Who they are and the values the school upholds
  will have a profound effect on the man your son becomes.
  You've got decisions to make about the sort of school that
  will suit your boy, as well as being aligned with your values.
  You've got state schools; Catholic schools; Steiner schools;
  schools of philosophy; Montessori schools; Jewish schools—
  even unschooling schools—to choose from. Some leading
  questions as you explore choices are: What environment
  suits my boy best? What's the school's philosophy? Do they
  have religious instruction and, if so, what sort? Is it what you
  want for your boy? How much emphasis is there on sport?
  The arts? How many male teachers does the school have?
  What's the playground space like? What are the rules? (See
  'Choosing a primary school' on page 86.)

Might is right

Some siblings are close from the get-go and others fight like caged cats. Mostly though, they seem to just nudge alongside each other and play happily enough . . . until at some mysterious point the worm turns and your lounge morphs into the Thunderdome—all flailing arms, screaming, flying missiles and wailing. The hardest question for parents is when is it time to intervene?

It's a difficult call, because kids find creative ways to annoy each other. There's the pointless baiting; for example, when they were either really bored or just to entertain themselves, two of our daughters would 'stare' at their brother until he cracked. 'Don't stare at me!' he'd yell at them. 'We're not doing anything,' they'd say, all doe-eyed. 'They *are* staring at me!' he'd moan to us. 'No we weren't.' Sort it out yourselves, we'd think!

Or when we were kids, I (Ruth) and my sister would spend hours bickering as we did the dishes (a now redundant activity!). 'This plate isn't clean,' the drier would say, putting it back in the sink to be rewashed. 'It was so!' the washer would yell, and on it would go until our parents, stretched to breaking point, would threaten to bang our heads together if we didn't stop!

Neither of these scenarios involved physical or emotional harm— it was more just incredibly annoying for anyone having to listen to them—so intervention wasn't really necessary. It's all part of sorting out pecking orders and testing out power by bossing the only person in the whole world kids are in control of—their younger sibling! It's when the ante is upped and bickering escalates into physical or emotional bullying (which can have longer-lasting effects) that it's time to step in and help them resolve the issue.

There are different drivers of bickering/fighting but they usually come down to:

- **Jealousy:** One kid perceives another is getting a better deal over something.
- **Competition over toys:** They want each other's things and don't always know how to share, or simply don't want to share at that particular time.
- **Competing for your attention:** Like jealousy, but maybe they are just feeling anxious for some reason and need more reassurance on that day.
- **Differing abilities:** The older child is trying to do or make something and although the younger sibling desperately wants in, they simply don't have the developmental ability to participate.
- **Personality differences:** One's easygoing and the other's an anxious perfectionist; trying to play or make something together is just a mismatch.
- **One of the kids is sick or tired:** Always worth checking out; kids can have short fuses when they're tired or unwell, just like adults.

Stepping into the conflict zone is a juggling act as you help teach your kids really important life skills about valuing another person's perspective, compromising and negotiating, and controlling aggressive impulses. Remember you are resolving the problem *with* them—not *for* them. Here are a few tips on how to do it:

- If they are beyond reason, separate them until they calm down (physically if you have to). Trying to talk when they're emotionally wired will only escalate the fight again. Tell them you'll help them sort it out when they've calmed down.

- Don't get stuck on trying to figure out which child is to blame—it takes two to tango and your goal is to help them both take responsibility for finding a solution to their problem.
- Start by encouraging them to say their piece without the other interrupting; one talks—one listens. Then change it out.
- Once they've listened to each other, try to help them find a 'win-win' situation, where they both feel like they've gained something; for example, if they are fighting over a toy, maybe they agree neither will play with it and they'll do something else together instead.
- Keep it short and sweet—don't thrash the issue. Boys, particularly, need clear agreements and boundaries.

You may also want to check out the environment—is there a lot of background noise from TV, radio or traffic? It's surprising how this can escalate tension. Try cutting down all background noise to help diffuse tensions.

Ultimately, your best weapon (irony accepted) in teaching your boy how to handle conflict is how you model it. He's watching you when you argue with your partner, the neighbour, your mother— soaking up how you resolve disagreements. The way you argue sets a strong example for your boy—if you are respectful, productive and not aggressive, chances are your son will adopt those tactics when he has issues. If he sees you routinely shout, slam doors and hurt others when you have problems, he'll likely model that.

Retrospectively, we fought too much in front of our kids, and it's presented them with challenges in their own adult relationships. We weren't violent but there was way too much yelling. If we'd known more about ourselves and our triggers, we'd have done it differently— taken time out, been better listeners, looked for compromises and solutions, been more forgiving. Just a heads-up, people.

Good eating

Once the 'arsenic hour'—that fabulous time of day when both children and parents are at home but dinner has not yet been served and things start to go bad—is becoming more manageable and your children have developed a bit more resilience, they are well able to take their place at the family dinner table and learn to eat largely what you do.

Research shows that children who eat the same food as their parents rather than having 'kids' meals' are far more likely to have healthy diets. In fact, eating adult meals is the most important determinant of a child's diet being healthy—far more so than whether they snack between meals, skip dinner or eat dinner on their laps in the living room in front of the TV.

Other research also shows the nutritional intake and growth rate of children between the ages of two and twelve can have a profound influence on their susceptibility to obesity and chronic diseases in later years. That's significant.

The authors of a British study which surveyed the eating habits of 2200 five-year-olds say its fine for busy parents to eat at a different time to their children—as long as the actual meal is always the same.

Dinner is also an important technology-device-free time, when kids learn the art of conversation through age-appropriate discussions.

You'll be amazed what they contribute once they know you value their thoughts, and you'll find out plenty about their worlds. Your sons will be learning the elements of one of civilisation's great triumphs— lunch- and dinnertime conversation!

So knock as much of the fussy eating on the head as you can. If your child has specific allergies it's easier to eliminate those foods from the whole family's diet, so you all eat much the same foods. If they are foods you love and don't want to give up, make them private treats outside of family meals.

Mealtimes are a chance to eyeball each other and find out what's on your kids' minds. What is your boy currently interested in? Are there any issues at school or problems he may need support with? A good conversation-starting tool is for the whole family to share 'highs and lows of the day'; for example, Mum's high: 'I sold two paintings at the gallery today—that felt good', and her low: 'There are more people begging on Queen St—I feel very sad for them.'

Bullying

Bullying happens. Despite parents condemning it and schools running anti-bullying programmes to combat it, it still goes on—be it physical, verbal or emotional. Bullying involves everything from broken bones and black eyes to crushing social exclusion. It's devastating when your child is the target and horrifying when you find out your kid is the perpetrator. Either way, you've got to get involved in making it stop. Because the truth is, the unrestricted school bully will likely grow into a violent adult, and the unprotected bullied kid will struggle to reach his potential.

Bullying 'involves a pattern of repeated aggressive behaviour with negative intent directed from one child to another where there is a power difference', according to Dr Dan Olweus, a Norwegian anti-bullying expert. It can happen between siblings, friends or kids at school. It is estimated 15 to 20 per cent of children are involved in bullying more than once or twice a term, either as bullies or victims.

As a parent, the hardest thing to handle about bullying is our reaction to it. Our primal instinct to protect our children makes us want to go out and hunt down the little horror who is bullying our kid and hurt them—badly. Public flogging wouldn't quite cut it! You want to do whatever it takes to make your child stop hurting. The trick is to use this protective impulse to support your boy to make the bullying stop—in partnership with him. Frame it as an opportunity for him to learn assertive skills to ground his self-confidence in action.

Your son may be reluctant to tell you he's being bullied; you may have to rely on clues like him becoming withdrawn or unusually angry. Does he have unexplained bruises, scratches or cuts? Is he suddenly reluctant to go to school and feigning illness? You know your boy best and you'll have to rely on your good knowledge of him to break through his silence. Trust your gut instincts—if you truly believe there's something wrong, listen to that feeling, because your son may fear reprisal if he 'tells' and believe that the consequences of 'telling' will be worse than the current situation. You'll need to reassure him that you believe him, you are going to help him to be safe and that the bullying is going to stop.

First of all, you'll need to gauge the extent of it: was it really bullying or an isolated act of aggression? That's important in terms of how you handle it, because if the behaviour was out of character for the perpetrator and he (or—increasingly—she) is remorseful, you are dealing with quite a different situation than ongoing bullying.

The things you need to know are:

- How long has it been going on?
- Is there just one perpetrator?
- How often does it happen, i.e. daily or weekly?
- Where does it happen?
- What happens?
- Has it escalated?
- What effect does it have on your boy?
- What has he tried doing/saying to stop it?
- Has he told anyone else about it?
- Have any friends tried to help him?

If you establish a pattern of bullying, it's time to take action. Start by talking through some strategies with your son, so he feels involved and empowered—the last thing you want is for him to feel more powerless. How does he feel about you going to school with him and talking to his teacher or the principal? What are his fears? What does he want to happen? Suggest going to visit the bully's parents—to talk it through and tell them and him what it feels like for your child. Then do it. You will need to show leadership here. Show him you're not scared.

Bullies lack what psychologists call pro-social behaviour—they don't know how to relate to others. Psychologist and author Steve Biddulph says in *Raising Boys* that in his experience, violent bullies are often hit a lot at home and 'have lost the natural reluctance that most children have to causing harm to others'. He writes that whole-school policies are the best solution to bullying. 'This means group discussions and teaching in the classroom about bullying, what it is, and that it is not okay.' He says the best methods involve not 'bullying the bully' but working with them and the children affected so they understand the hurt they are causing. 'Discussion methods have a big advantage over punishment in that they don't drive the problem underground or escalate it by making the bully more excluded or more of a social failure.'

If it turns out your boy is doing the bullying, he needs your help too. If you know it's not coming from the home—i.e. he's not witnessing or experiencing violence there—engage with him to find out what's driving this behaviour that is clearly unacceptable to you. Let him know you don't approve of or condone his behaviour—without shaming him. Be very clear it's his behaviour you dislike, not him. Rather than saying 'I am disappointed in you', try 'I know this is not the best of you' or 'I know you are better than this, bigger than this sort of behaviour'. Call to his higher self.

Because if all he feels is shame, rather than remorse, he's missed out on a much-needed lesson in empathy. Then take him to meet the victim's parents and get him to apologise to the victim.

Because chronic bullying can have profound, lifelong impacts on children, if it's so bad it can't be easily resolved with either your or his school's intervention, consider pulling your boy out of the school. This is serious stuff—don't muck around and let it slide. Find a school that has more rigorous anti-bullying policies.

Interestingly, one Auckland school that loosened up its playground rules as part of a university research project found bullying markedly decreased—an unexpected result. Swanson Primary School principal Bruce McLachlan told the *Sunday Star-Times*: 'The kids were motivated, busy and engaged. In my experience, the time children get into trouble is when they are not busy, motivated and engaged. It's during that time they bully other kids, graffiti or wreck things around the school.' (See 'Choosing a primary school' on page 86.)

Weapons of mass destruction

Boys and weapons, eh? Many of us who came up through the hippy peace movement of the 1960 and 1970s were reluctant to give our precious children guns or swords because weapons were not part of our peace lexicon; one of our first children wasn't even put in a cot because it had bars! That worked out well (not)! We'd watched parents and grandparents scarred by war and decided no weapons for our kids—we wove flowers in our hair and sang songs of freedom as we protested against the Vietnam War (1955–73) and raised wild children free from violence. But they found weapons anyway. They made swords out of sticks and guns out of pegs—one friend's son chewed himself a gun out of a piece of toast!

So what drives boys to want to play with guns and swords and make annoying weapon noises? Is it primal? And the question we get asked by mothers a lot: will my boy turn out to be a violent psychopath if I let him have a toy gun or play with a sword?

Studies show that boys and girls have different styles of play, especially between the ages of three and six. Psychologists suggest boys gravitate more toward active play with themes of fighting and weaponry. Whether this is a conditioned difference is debatable—all we can do is work with what is there and try to ease parents' fears about their sons wanting to play with weapons.

At a basic level, boys strongly associate with superheroes—many of them toting weapons—as a way of identifying with bravery. These invincible superheroes don't shy away from danger and they use their attributes for good in the world—the old story of good triumphing over evil. These are positive values.

If we accept that assertiveness and aggression are natural instincts that we need to 'socialise'—i.e. find pro-social ways to express without hurting others—then playing with toy swords and guns can allow your boy to 'play' with aggression, as a way towards integrating these feelings in a healthy way.

Guns teach the basic 'point and shoot' of achievement thinking, i.e. set your goal (target), focus on it and apply yourself to that target. Swordplay also builds good foundations for the 'cut and thrust' of debate when he's older, of clear, decisive thinking. You hear this in our language: 'cut out the bullshit' and 'cut through the crap'. Personally, we think spears beat guns hands down in teaching these lessons because boys also learn the limits of their power and influence.

There's a big difference between aggressive play and aggressive behaviour. If there's a real intent to harm—or if your son can't resolve conflict except through overpowering other kids—then sure, you've got a problem and it's time to put down the guns and start talking.

But do we think playing with toy guns and swords creates psychopaths? Nah. It takes a lot more than that to grow a person capable of deliberately harming others without remorse. According to Dr Scott Bonn, professor of sociology and criminology at Drew University in New Jersey in the United States, psychopathy is related to a genetic physiological defect that results in the underdevelopment of the part of the brain responsible for impulse control and emotions (as opposed to sociopathy, which is attributed to 'nurture', i.e. social isolation, abuse and/or neglect, etc.).

In *The Moral Molecule: The New Science of What Makes Us Good or Evil*, Paul J. Zak says psychopaths are often remarkable for their high intelligence, but their lack of empathy allows them to treat others as objects. Their cognitive skills enable them to get away with this behaviour.

The good news is there are no large-scale studies linking fake guns and other weaponry to real-life aggression—in fact, research shows there are much stronger indicators of psychopathy in young people, such as cruelty to animals or hurting people just for the sake of it.

Interestingly, we knew one committed pacifist father whose son was obsessed by guns. While visiting America, this guy took his son to a gun range and let him fulfil his dream to shoot a machine gun. To balance out the experience, he then he took him to a rehabilitation centre filled with people who had been wounded by gunshots. That boy is now an internationally recognised photographer—there was a point to him learning to be an accurate shooter!

What we say about the weaponry of boyhood is try to keep it basic—leave as much up to your son's imagination as possible. An ultra-realistic machine gun with all the lights and noises doesn't leave much room for your son's imagination. It should be his imagination doing the work of 'playing with aggression'. Spears made from flax stalks or toetoe; swords invented from sticks or wood; guns created from pointed fingers or simple wooden toy guns will all do the business. Water pistols are great too and, later, catapults and shanghais under supervision.

Ancestor worship

Your son needs to know something about the long line of ancestors he comes from—particularly the men. Notice traits or features in him, mannerisms that are family likenesses. Who is he like? Does he remind you of a grandparent or uncle? Is it the way he laughs? His sense of humour? The way he thinks? Tell him, 'Your granddad dances just like you'—he may not respond much at this age but deeper down, you are helping him build connections to his ancestors and seeding anchors that will inform and support him in adulthood.

While your boy is an emerging personality—not a formed one, regardless of similarities to others—you don't want to pigeonhole kids by labelling them, through a misguided desire to place them in the family before they are ready to take their place in it. However, we do think it's important to link your boy into a family lineage that anchors his place in the world—without confining him to being a mini-me or replica of who he resembles, of course!

Excluding Maori, who have been in New Zealand for thousands of years, we are a relatively young country. Most migrants have broken family ties, often living without grandparents, aunts, uncles and cousins. While this dislocation affords everyone the chance of re-creating themselves—free from the constrictions of often rigid family and cultural structures—it also leaves a void that makes it challenging to form a strong sense of self. It's the old 'If you don't know where you came from, you don't know where you are going' theory.

It is rich family stories that help us build a strong platform to stand on. Knowing the strengths and weaknesses of our ancestors enables us to build on the best traits and avoid the worst excesses—like alcoholism, for example. Even knowing bad stuff affords us an honesty that we can live with. Someone we know recently found out their great-grandfather, who was rarely spoken of, committed suicide on board a ship coming back from the Australian goldfields in the late 1800s. He couldn't face the defeat of returning home empty-handed. This filled in all sorts of missing pieces for our friend, who researched the shame associated with suicide back then and had a much better understanding of her grandfather and father.

Knowing your ancestors can also be a good anchor for a boy to make a connection to an ancestor he respects, admires or even considers a hero. It's the specific quality that the boy admires in the ancestor that counts, rather than the person, for example: 'Your granddad made people laugh—everybody loved him' or 'Your great uncle was a wonderful musician', etc. To make ancestor worship useful it's important that your boy links it to the qualities of the hero and then links those qualities to those emerging in himself. (See 'Oh Superman' below.)

Ferret out those family photos and stories and share them with your boy. They don't have to be long or involved; just give him snippets of his lineage—the good and the bad. And remember, it's the stories that inform more than the facts.

Oh Superman

Some people shine a light that shows you who you could be. That's what heroes do—they don't have to be famous or rich, but they do need to possess qualities you aspire to. When you look at them you think, 'I want to be just like him (or her)'. Their qualities could include honesty, bravery, loyalty, strength, intelligence, courage, self-sacrifice, determination, tenacity, compassion, empathy, focus, dedication, creativity, perseverance and wisdom.

These are fundamental qualities we all possess to greater or lesser degrees, but what sets a hero apart from the rest of us riff-raff is that he or she can be said to be the highest or the most perfect embodiment of these virtues. They give us something to strive for—the hope being that by emulating our heroes we will become fabulous people who contribute to the world in meaningful rather than destructive ways.

A hero's role is 'to protect and to serve', so a hero has to be willing to sacrifice his own needs on behalf of others. His quest is really the search for identity and wholeness, and above and beyond the physical challenges he faces, a hero must also come to terms with himself; he must change and grow. He has to take risks to reap rewards—that's a fundamental requirement of being a hero.

The most well-known heroic archetypes for boys are the King, the Warrior, the Magician and the Lover. These were described by Swiss psychiatrist and psychotherapist Carl Jung (1875–1961), following on from Austrian neurologist Sigmund Freud (1856–1939) and his work on how mythological forces in the unconscious mind shape our individual personalities. American mythologist Joseph Campbell (1904–1987) expanded on this theory to develop the concept of 'the hero's journey'—where the naïve hero identifies a big dilemma, embarks on an adventure or quest to sort it out, finds a mentor along the way to guide him, goes through all sorts of trials and tests to overcome the situation, faces death on the way back with the treasure (or solution) and finally returns home a hero, having achieved great deeds on behalf of the group, tribe or civilisation in general. A big day out!

We see this archetypal scenario played out in many of our fictional heroes—from old Greek ones like Trojan leader Hector to Luke Skywalker in *Star Wars*, Frodo Baggins in *Lord of the Rings*, Clark Kent in various iterations of Superman or young wizard Harry Potter. They all had to put on their big-boy boots and head off on various quests to overcome evil. Some of them—like Superman—never get out of the loop!

These heroic images and narratives play an important part in laying down the soil of character development in boyhood. They say, 'This is what the culture is offering you as archetypal aspirational figures.' Today in New Zealand, boys are mainly offered the warrior archetype through sports—generally rugby—by way of the player who can overcome significant physical and psychological challenges and survive a lot of pain to achieve a successful end result.

Famous ex-All Black Frank Bunce told us he's embarrassed by the way students hero-worship him when he goes into schools as a role model, because he believes he got to become an All Black through hard work and discipline, rather than through heroic deeds. Frank is a great supporter of the work we do at Big Buddy because he says our mentors are still there after the rugby season finishes—week after week after week. It's that ongoing support and praise, rather than trying to achieve heroic status, that really raises aspirations and achievement, he says.

Luckily, there are lots of other archetypes our boys can aspire to— environmental activists or eco-warriors, for example, in our opinion, are a wonderful translation of the same concept. They aim to look after and protect the community; protect the earth. They are warriors because their actions are heroic—they risk life and limb climbing onto Japanese whaling boats in the Southern Ocean, for example; they overcome incredible odds, battling against corporations; they get arrested, and have enemies trying to take them down.

These aspirational, archetypal images do awaken something in boys. We fully support them throwing on their Superman capes and going after supervillain Lex Luthor, but heroic images come and go in boys. They can't be walking around school on a daily basis with a sword trying to save the world—they need a much wider set of skills. That's why we're more interested in boys having an ongoing relationship with a real hero—preferably their father—who has already made the journey into adulthood and can model the best of the heroic qualities, such as honesty, loyalty, intelligence, courage, sacrifice, compassion, empathy, perseverance and wisdom. If boys don't have these real men—with real flaws—in their lives, they will continue to look out to the unreachable heroes in the world, which can make them feel isolated and not good enough.

Ultimately, all the swords and capes and guns and mimicking heroes is about making the journey into manhood. The trick is to balance the heroic archetypes with praise for the smaller things your boy achieves that will raise his sense of self-worth—as opposed to raising his self-esteem, which is giving him the message he can be and do anything he wants, which simply isn't true. Self-worth is about accepting yourself for everything you are, including what you *can't* do. Having an ongoing relationship with a regular bloke—a real superhero—means boys are going to see all that guy's flaws as well as his obvious strengths. (See 'The difference between self-worth and self-esteem' on page 76.)

Having a relationship like this will help to open up your boy's eyes beyond the archetypes that are being thrown at him by popular culture—mainly driven by commercial interests. Let's face it, you don't see a lot of reinforcing images for boys to become poets, writers, artists or dancers!

Following a boy's interests, as they emerge week after week in an ongoing relationship, we encourage our mentors to look at what is growing in the boy—if a dancer's emerging, find other dancers for him to model off! Don't saddle him with exposure to limited warrior archetypes that see him forever trying to model the tough macho archetype that he is not and will never be.

Make sure he gets exposure to a wider range of heroes than the warrior, for example:

- **Kings:** Wise decision-makers, leaders we respect, who we are willing to follow. Think great leaders in history, kings and princes you admire, local community leaders.
- **Magicians:** Those heroes that create something out of nothing or solve problems just by thinking better than the rest of us, e.g. computer programmers, creative artists, intellectuals, inventors, craftspeople and stage magicians.
- **Lovers:** Those who empathise with the trials and tribulations of others and care for them, e.g. nurses, doctors, counsellors, social workers, those working with people in poverty, etc.

Praise is gold

It's about now we need to talk about praise. Because authentic praise is like gold to boys—they need it almost as much as they need food. In fact, it's like soul food to them.

Praise sits at the heart of what we do at Big Buddy. We encourage our mentors to be real and authentic with their praise—notice the small things they can affirm in the boys they mentor and praise them without being effusive. We really encourage you to do the same—not just with your own son but with any boys who cross your path. We're talking very small praise here: a nod of the head; the classic Kiwi raising of the eyebrows; or 'I like your shoes'. Leave it there and trust it's enough. That's the real beauty of praise—like a great perfume, you need very little to make a big impact!

Praise—especially from an older man—is so valuable to boys because it's part of how they form their masculine identity. Acknowledgement from older males tells boys what they are doing is approved of; that they are on track to becoming a good man. It's a continual welcoming into the Man Tribe.

Sorry, mums, but there is a difference between praise from a woman and praise from a man. We're not saying either has higher or lower value—it's just more potent coming from a man because your boy identifies as male.

Most of the boys we see know their mothers love them—it's like a foundation rock for them. Adult men will talk about their mothers as being akin to Mary, Mother of God—they have absolute faith they are loved by their mums.

The vulnerability men—and boys as they are growing up—have is that they need acknowledgement of their male gender through praise, and a mother can't do that. It doesn't mean anything for a boy to be praised for his masculine stuff by a woman, because she's not in the tribe.

We have a phrase for times when a man gives the slightest amount of praise to a boy and it shifts things radically—a 'mentoring moment'. The classic praise we talk about in our training—and all men get it—is the slight lift of the eyebrows. So if, for example, your boy puts the bait on his hook without cutting his fingers, just raise your eyebrows slightly or nod your head—you don't need to say anything—and there is a little gold moment of praise where your boy's sense of himself swells up because has been affirmed by a man that what he has done is good. It affirms his identity as boy/man. Boys are like dogs that want to please—they want to get it right—and they are fascinated by this male stuff.

But whatever you do, avoid the tyranny of 'awesome'—never has a word been so overused! The marketing machine out there works 'awesome' mercilessly—they try to sell it to boys that they'll be better men—awesome, even—if they wear this kind of basketball shirt, or these boots, or have this hairstyle, or play this video game, or be an All Black—there are all sorts of images of what malehood should be. So calm down, folks, and hold back on the 'awesomes'; explore the myriad of more subtle ways to praise your boy before resorting to 'You're awesome'.

Boys are fascinated with 'Who am I?' and 'Who should I be?'. There's no shortage of competing images about who they could/ should be, but when a real flesh-and-blood person—particularly a man—affirms their actions, their behaviour or their being by praising them, it's feedback; they're getting something right.

You don't have to look for something to praise in your boy—just be open to noticing it. We strongly encourage you to be authentic with your praise—avoid any 'I'd better praise the boy now' impulses and 'Well done—you're amazing. You'll be a prime minister one day' bollocks. Boys know false praise when they hear it—they know it's not true and all it will do is set them up for failure. False praise gives boys a false sense of confidence and helps breed people who believe their own bullshit. It breeds people with 'high self-esteem—low self-worth', according to Auckland psychologist John Bryant. You know them when you meet them because their abilities are way out of whack with their high opinion of themselves!

What we see from the outside is how long praise lasts. Authentic praise for doing something well will last a boy for weeks. The classic story is of a mentor who took his boy out on a boat at his fishing club; the boy won a fishing rod for catching the snapper of the day.

That boy was walking on air for weeks. And these were real Kiwi blokes, remember; they weren't effusing, 'Yay! You're the best—you're the champion!'—none of that bollocks! Just bloke stuff like 'Well done, mate—you got the best snapper'—then moving on. Because that boy knew those blokes didn't give praise lightly, he knew it was the real shit and that's the gold. It boosted his self-worth, rather than his self-esteem.

Another fishing story from the Big Buddy files illustrates how simple yet subtle authentic praise can be. We had a mentor whose Little Buddy's passion was fishing, so he took him out. Neither of them talked much—just functional stuff—but the mentor did the head nod when the boy cast his line right. Next weekend they did the same thing, but this time the boy caught a small fish. The mentor gave him the nod again. The mentor rang us, saying he was really worried because they weren't communicating much—he thought he was failing. But when we rang the mother, she was thrilled—said the boy was over the moon when he came home; said he'd had the best day of his life! The nod was enough.

Sometimes praise is so small; just a guy showing up in a boy's life says to him, 'I said I would. Here I am. Let's go fishing.' It increases the boy's self-worth because that man is saying, 'You're important enough for me to turn up for.' That's sufficient—it's as simple as that. 'You matter to me. I'm not being told to do this; there are other things I could be doing but I'm choosing to take you fishing.' It directly affirms self-worth.

The difference between self-worth and self-esteem

We've talked about the tyranny of 'awesome' and how it breeds high self-esteem but low self-worth. Self-esteem is how you present yourself to other people, and self-worth is how you actually feel about yourself; a bit like the difference between the clothes you choose to wear and your skin. Our opinion on this issue is based on evidence from interviews with over 650 men who have applied to become Big Buddy mentors. During these in-depth interviews we see what manifests in manhood that has gone wrong in boyhood, and the building of self-esteem that is not matched by ability is one of them. We put this down to false praise.

Up until about the 1950s or 1960s, when Sigmund Freud's psychoanalysis theories started to take hold in Western countries, praise was largely reserved for God. It was thought children would become big-headed if they were praised too much—above God, as it were. In many places, such as China and Japan, that worry about 'inflating the ego' means praise is still rare.

But in the West, having discovered through psychoanalysis that deep emotional scars could be attributed in part to war-damaged parents who were scant on praising their children, the worm slowly turned. Westerners began the slow march into lavishing praise on their children. The belief was that praise would make kids better— more motivated, more confident, more inclined to tackle challenges.

The praise volume seems to have ramped up—in the 1970s it was 'You're great'; in the 1980s 'You're a winner—everyone's a winner'; and by the 1990s 'You can do anything' became the motivational catch-cry. But that didn't really help kids succeed either so we had to keep ramping up the adjectives. Now everyone and everything is 'amazing' and 'awesome'! Where will it go now? What's after awesome?

We think the tyranny of awesome lays a huge responsibility on boys. In reality, only one in about four million people is going to be the prime minister; the chances are remote. And besides, you don't have to be awesome to be a prime minister—you just have to be clever.

You don't want to raise a boy with high self-esteem and low self-worth, because he's going to stuff up every which way as he painstakingly learns the humbling reality that he, too, is a flawed human being.

Boundary setting

Monday afternoon is 'Granny Day' in our family. This involves Granny (Ruth) picking up Mr Four-year-old from day-care and Miss Seven-year-old from school before taking them home, where the whole family gathers for a shared meal. It's a good gig—regular for the kids and a great time to all get together and catch up on our busy lives.

What this regular weekly rhythm does is allows us to watch our grandkids' cognitive and physical skills develop over time. Because we don't have responsibility for their day-to-day care, we're not hooked into them in the way their parents are, and can observe behaviours without reacting to them. It's a wonderful thing!

We noticed when Mr Recently-turned-four made a giant leap for mankind. He could hear the word 'no' without throwing himself on the floor and wailing like a stuck pig! Up until then, his underdeveloped frontal cortex meant he simply didn't have the ability to handle setbacks or to self-regulate without reacting (his impulse control will remain a work in progress until his frontal cortex is fully developed by about the age of 25). An improvement in his cognitive and physical skills means he can now handle tasks more easily and doesn't get so frustrated. Less frustration equals greater self-control and fewer tantrums. Boundaries are much easier to set and enforce and the whole household is happier for it.

From the age of four onwards you can begin establishing rules and using tools such as positive reinforcement, redirecting their attention, giving more verbal instructions/explanations, using time out, grounding and withholding privileges. Your boy is able to grasp this level of cognitive boundary-setting and will begin to respond really well to it. One: boys love boundaries because they make them feel safe; and two, he wants to please you (well, most of the time anyway!).

However, it's fair to say boundary-setting is the most challenging aspect of parenting. Just when you think you've sorted out an annoying behaviour and everyone is on the same page, your boy kicks off with a new one. The long road to the age of four and emergent reasoning will test every ounce of your self-control and knowledge as your boy pushes boundaries you hadn't even thought of. It's worth remembering; as *Huffington Post* parenting blogger Sarah MacLaughlin writes—'Raising children is a marathon—not a sprint.'

'When your child behaves in a rude or unsafe manner and your fuse has gotten short, emotions will run high. In the worst of these scenarios, your amygdala hijacks your prefrontal cortex and floods your body with adrenalin and cortisol, sending you into fight-or-flight mode. At this point, you are no longer a rational human,' writes MacLaughlin, who also wrote *What Not to Say: Tools for Talking with Young Children*—a succinct guide that shows busy parents, teachers, relatives and caregivers how to revamp their communication with one- to six-year-olds.

Psychiatrist and mindful-parenting advocate Dr Dan Siegel talks about the 'downstairs' and 'upstairs' brain. Once the downstairs brain has taken over, within two to three seconds you have lost control and go from being a sort of reasonable human being to 'flipping your lid'. You've joined your boy in the Thunderdome and all hell breaks loose. No one is in control at that point. We all know this place and it doesn't feel good!

The trick, says Dr Siegel, is to regain control through mindfulness. Step back, take some deep breaths and begin regulating your responses by figuring out what's happening for you. Why are you having such a big reaction—why is this situation pushing your buttons? If, for example, your son is having a meltdown because he was sidelined—again—during rugby practice at school, and it makes you really angry too, ask yourself why? Does it trigger memories for you of being left out of things at school? Have you recently been unfairly disciplined at work for someone else's mistake? It's important you understand your own emotional drivers so you can help your son deal with the situation he's facing. 'Attunement is the gateway to compassion and empathy,' writes Siegel. And we agree: your son needs your understanding and help—not your unconscious emotional response that has nothing to do with him.

It almost goes without saying (but we will say it anyway) that you will probably initially fail miserably at this mindfulness exercise. Our four children will certainly attest to this! But remember, practice makes perfect—the more you try to get in touch with your emotional responses before you react, the faster you'll become at it.

We've elaborated here on MacLaughlin's best tips for boundary-setting:

- **Think ahead—make a plan and be strategic:** You have to be one step ahead. You're the adult, so you often know the places where your kids will push or fall apart.

- **Don't use wishy-washy language:** Aim to eliminate statements like 'I don't really want you to do that' (no, really?) and the ubiquitous 'OK?' at the end of your sentences. Say it like you mean it. 'We do not do that in this house.'

- **Check your body language and facial expression:** Non-verbal cues carry huge importance. Don't go all sing-songy if you mean business. And always, always, *always* get low. He'll know you mean business when you are crouched down close to your boy and wearing a neutral facial expression.

- **Ensure that your tone is warm, but firm:** A sharp tone or staccato cadence can be over-stimulating and scary to a young child, setting off their fight-or-flight alarm. Yelling will trigger this as well—save it for emergencies. Consciously lower your voice—think bass, not soprano.

- **Don't expect a child to comply without upset:** Set the limit where the limit is for you. Then make space for the feelings. It is unrealistic to expect a child to accept 'No' with, 'OK, sure.' That will rarely happen. But it will happen more if you are calm and reassuring: 'Yes, I see you are upset but I said no and I mean no.' Bottom line, don't expect your boy to agree with or affirm you here. You are the grown-up—stay strong.

- **Have developmentally appropriate expectations:** One-year-olds get into everything. Two-year-olds cannot share without protest. Three-year-olds will say 'no' often. Four-year-olds must know 'why'. Five-year-olds can be quite sassy, and on it goes. Brush up on where your child is at developmentally.

- **Stay decisive, even when you change your mind:** Confidence in your decisions is crucial. Staying consistent in your decisiveness is way more important than a rule being unwavering. You may feel guilty, but don't let guilt wobble your resolve.

- **Be physical if you need to:** Unless you are feeling really frustrated, it is OK to corral a child physically to keep them (or others) safe. Holding them in your lap facing outward (so you don't get hurt either) is a useful way to do this. Check in with yourself and stay calm—*never* touch your child when you are angry.

- **Don't explain the reason for the limit more than once:** It can be helpful to give the reason for the limit but do not repeat yourself; it will only irritate you. Offer the explanation once, then keep quiet. Remember, it's an explanation in simple language, not a justification.

- **Use humour:** We cannot stress enough how well this works. Animate, and imbue with wit, objects like the toothbrush or bathtub water (seriously!). Try a silly voice or tone, or invent a wild character. The Commanding Queen or Bossy Sergeant work quite well! Try using it before things escalate.

- **Pick your battles:** Stop and ask yourself if the situation is worth the battle. Does it really matter? So he's used the last of the bread to make a bird trap without asking you. Let it go. As long as you are being largely consistent with your boundary-setting, save your energy for when it really matters.

- **Life isn't fair:** Kids have different personalities and needs and respond to discipline accordingly. You need to be consistent but that doesn't mean one size fits all. Fairness is when everyone gets what they need—not when everyone gets the same thing.

Hothousing is bollocks

This might be challenging, but we're going to say it anyway—hothousing your boy is a waste of time. In fact, we'd go as far as saying it can harm him, contributing to performance anxiety and abnormal socialisation if he's catapulted out of his social cohort.

By hot-housing, we mean bringing academic education and physical training into your boy's life early. For example, teaching him to read before he goes to school in the misguided belief he will do better educationally, or teaching him the violin at the age of two, in the hope he will be concert violinist at 12.

It won't make an iota of difference to his education or career prospects; all you'll do is rob him of the valuable playtime he needs to learn the socialisation and emotional skills he'll require to become a good, happy man.

Even though parents think it's important for their kids to learn cognitive skills like colours and numbers, etc., research shows that it doesn't have any long-term benefits: early cognitive stimulation (before the age of about seven) is not a predictor of later success, e.g. gaining a degree.

Parenting educator and Brainwave Trust lead trainer Nathan Mikaere-Wallis said in a Radio New Zealand National interview that how a child feels about themselves as a learner is the most important thing. 'An eight-year-old who learned to read at three and a half years has the same reading age typically as a kid who learned to read at six and a half years—there's simply no advantage.'

Think of it like the hot-housing of plants—they grow really fast and big but they're not necessarily nutritious. Take the hot-house and stimulants away and they wither and die. What we're looking for with parenting is to make good compost—fertile soil that creates a love of learning. The essence of that soil is curiosity and imagination and that is not learned by training; it's encouraged by play, by tinkering with things and ideas.

'Help build up their perception of themselves as good learners,' advised Mikaere-Wallis. 'The more we encourage kids to direct their own learning, the better they'll do. If they are confident in their ability to learn, their enthusiasm for new learning is self-generated.'

He said building intelligence is all about risk-taking. When we push children it tends to inhibit risk-taking.

'It's important not to correct kids too much when they get something wrong. Just model the correct response. Here's a good example: my son says to me in the car, "I can see the sheeps". Instead of correcting him, I say, "I can see the sheep too".'

A lot of boys—even ones who have loved day-care—struggle to settle into the structure of school and maybe the truth is they're not ready for it. There's starting to be a lot of debate around this. In most Western countries kids start school at six, based on Jean Piaget's theory of cognitive development. Before Piaget developed his theory in the mid-1900s, the thinking was basically that children were little adults who learned in the same way as adults—just less competently. But Piaget's research turned this theory on its ear, proving that children's brains were strikingly different from those of adults. He established that the brain was not developed enough for children to begin cognitive learning until the age of six.

But in New Zealand we still start them at five. This goes back to World War I, when most Western countries lowered the school starting-age to five so more women could work while so many men were fighting in Europe. Unfortunately, because of the huge losses New Zealand suffered—almost 17,000 killed and more than 41,000 wounded—when most other Western countries put the school starting-age back up to six after the war, we didn't. With 5 per cent of all our men of military age killed, we still had a labour shortage after the war and needed kids at school so more adults could work.

Mikaere-Wallis said in the Radio New Zealand National interview that this has created all sorts of educational distortions, for boys particularly, like the need for remedial reading programmes. 'We make them wrong from the get-go. Asking boys to do something from five that they can't possibly do just disables their learning. How are they gonna feel about themselves? Boys just want to keep playing!'

Our view is that it's our job as parents to help our boys grow into confident, happy men by creating environments they will flourish in, rather than setting them up for failure in often archaic, poorly designed educational systems that stymie their creativity and limit their potential. This is not always the case, granted, but it happens enough to negatively impact educational outcomes for boys. (See 'Choosing a primary school' on page 86.)

How to help your boy learn

- Create the thinker before you put the facts in.
- Good outcomes are associated with less structure.
- Think fun and interesting.
- Have a high quality relationship.

—Nathan Mikaere-Wallis, neuroscience expert

Choosing a primary school

The world your child is going to inhabit as an adult will be radically different to the one you live in now. For starters, many jobs you know now will be lost to automation. In fact, within the next 20 years there's a 50/50 chance a robot will steal your job. Traditional blue-collar jobs like driving and labouring are likely to be the first to go, but white-collar professions like accountancy and administration are in the firing line as well.

And if that isn't enough to get your head around, consider this: by 2038, Auckland's ethnic makeup with be 11.4 per cent Maori; 15.7 per cent Pacific; 30.6 per cent Asian and 42.3 per cent European and 'other'. By 2041 the population of New Zealand will be over 6 million and almost 2 million people will be over 65. Welcome to your son's ethnically diverse and aging future!

According to *The Superdiversity Stocktake* report by Mai Chen, chairwoman of the Superdiversity Centre of Law, Policy and Business, the change will take longer to reach the regions, with some class-rooms in Otago and Southland remaining predominantly European. But it will happen, and our education system is going to need a major overhaul to cope with the diversity tsunami coming our way.

For example, within the next six years, 20,000 children in Auckland are expected to be learning Mandarin. That's a big shift from the tiny percentage of us working-class baby-boomers who pointlessly learned French when we were at school! This also has significant implications for the biculturalism that sits at the heart of both our cultural identity and institutions, but that's a whole other discussion.

So, keeping in mind the whole employment and ethnic landscape will be radically different in the not-too-distant future, you've got some thinking to do about what kind of education you want for your boy. There will be new jobs and careers we can only imagine, so gone are the days when schooling was training for a known job.

You may also want to consider whether he's ready for school at five, or if it would be better for him to start when he turns six—which you are legally allowed to do. As mentioned above, this is in line with most European countries: 20 out of 34 European countries have a school starting-age of six, while another eight wait until children are seven. In the US and the UK, kids start at between four and six. There's a lot of research to support this approach.

From a developmental perspective, boys' brains are six to twelve months behind girls'. This shows up primarily in the area of fine motor skills; for example, their ability to hold pencils or use scissors. In *Raising Boys*, author Steve Biddulph writes that because boys are also still in the stage of gross motor development, developing nerves to their bigger arm, leg and body muscles, they will be 'itching to move their bodies around—they'll struggle to sit still'.

'In fact, until they finish their gross motor development, they will not gain fine motor skills. For boys, one leads to the other. Girls do it in reverse: their brains go straight to finger coordination and they often need help in body strengthening.'

The fear of keeping your boy back from starting school for a year is, of course, that he'll be a year behind for the rest of his life. This simply isn't true. A 2010 US study found school entry-age had no effect on wages, employment, home ownership, household income or marital status as an adult. He'll be just fine.

Del McFarlane-Scott, deputy principal at Ranui Primary School in Auckland, says the major problem time with boys at school is around 11am, when everyone comes in from morning tea. 'There's a lot of testosterone happening at the door and settling to learn is a real issue. We need to look at what they are doing out in the playground and set them up to succeed at learning when they come back into the classroom.'

McFarlane-Scott, who also has three sons and seven grandsons, says boys need to run around every 20 minutes or so, so she encourages teachers to regularly get them up and running around the playground to calm them down enough to learn. She says a lot of boys don't get enough activity at home—spending too much time sitting with iPads or phones, etc., playing games. 'I see them at school on the computers and they're almost twitching with physicality—we just send them outside. If they bring that level of tenseness into the classroom they become unteachable.'

She says boys like a beginning, middle and an end to their learning. 'They want to know what the task is, what you want at the finish, and they need to know they've completed it. Then they're off to play. Girls are happy to have an activity, go off and do something else and come back to it later. So, longer projects are awesome for girls—but really frustrating for boys.'

Boys also experience delays in language development and are twice as likely as girls to develop literacy and behaviour problems. McFarlane-Scott says all the children on behaviour programmes at her school are boys. 'In fact, all the children who are under-achieving are boys. We're asking ourselves is it a problem with the boys? Or is it something we need to be doing differently to better meet their needs? That's the challenge.'

In *Raising Boys*, Biddulph is harsh in his summing up of schooling for boys: 'The learning environment of schools seems designed to educate senior citizens, not young people at their most energetic.

Everyone is supposed to be quiet, nice and compliant.' He recommends parents look at their child and think not 'How old is he?' but 'Is he ready for school?' In boys' cases, the answer is often: not yet.

Warwick Pudney—a passionate men's advocate, author, former teacher and currently a senior lecturer at Auckland University of Technology—runs workshops for teachers looking at the difference between girls' and boys' learning, why boys achieve at a lower level than girls, and how to make education boy-friendly. Pudney, who was an original founder of the Big Buddy programme, says on a Learning Network NZ YouTube video that the fact that male achievement at university level is up to 50 per cent lower than female is something that should concern us all. We agree.

If you decide your son is ready for school, you've got some decisions to make that may include:

- **Should he attend the local school?** Going to a nearby school will ensure he is well socialised into his local community. Outside of school, he'll play with the kids he goes to school with. You'll get to know the other parents in your neighbourhood, which will help when he hits the challenging teenage years and starts to branch out. The downsides are your local school may not provide the type of education you want for your son, for a number of reasons.
- **Should he go to an all-boys school or co-ed?** There are pros and cons to both. He's likely to do better educationally at an all-boys school because he's not competing with (or trying to impress) girls and he'll be more focused academically. If he does go to an all-boys school, make sure he has regular contact with girls and women—he's going to

have to share the world with them. At a co-ed school, he's likely to get a more rounded education—gaining much-needed interpersonal skills like empathy and compassion that will serve him well in the increasingly cooperative work world he will inhabit.

- **What kind of school will he flourish in?** Once again, you'll have to take a really good look at your boy and decide what kind of environment he grows well in. You'll need to look at things like how big the playground is, what sort of rules they have and how many rules there are. Some schools are really loosening up their playground rules, with a resultant drop in bullying and better focus in the classroom, especially for boys.

- **Does the school have boys-only classes?** There's a movement towards this segregation, with co-ed primary schools such as Waitakere Primary in West Auckland and Belmont Primary on Auckland's North Shore getting positive results from splitting off the boys and implementing more boy-friendly teaching strategies like more active and shorter-burst learning.

- **Is a spiritual or religious educational component important to you?** If so, you'll have to explore what's on offer. New Zealand state schools are largely secular but depending on your particular beliefs, you can look at Kura Kaupapa Maori, Catholic or other Christian, Jewish, Steiner/Waldorf, Muslim, School of Philosophy, Buddhist, etc., alternatives.

Many of the mentors we interview at Big Buddy report struggling at school. They tell us it didn't really work for them, it didn't make much sense; and yet they are quite successful adults—they managed to carve out good careers, despite the challenges of the education system. They don't talk much about academic achievement—more about the social environment and how they fitted in. So it's good to keep in mind that while schools run an academic curriculum, a huge part of the learning going on is about social interaction—what happens in the playground.

McFarlane-Scott says it's really important for boys to know what the pecking order or hierarchy is and where they fit in it. 'They sort that out and then generally, they're ready to learn. With girls, it's more like a spider's web of relationships.

'And boys are very black and white—there's no grey. Things are either right or wrong—you're the boss or I'm the boss. What you see is what you get with boys, whereas girls are more complicated—a lot more goes on emotionally. Boys need strong relationships—a strong role model—to keep them motivated at school. We try to put those role models in front of them.'

The ADHD debate

Does he have ADHD or is he just a very busy boy? The term attention deficit hyperactivity disorder was first coined in 1980 for what has become a very controversial 'condition'. The number (including adults) being prescribed medication for ADHD in New Zealand grows year on year—from 98,000 in 2005 to 144,000 in 2013.

Between 3 and 5 per cent of children are estimated to have ADHD—that equates to one in every class of 20 students and approximately 25 kids in a school of 500. That's a hell of a lot of kids! In the US, one in 10 children is labelled ADHD and boys are three times more likely than girls to be diagnosed. ADHD often goes hand in hand with other child mental health problems such as depression and/or anxiety. Most ADHD children have the social and emotional maturity of children two-thirds their age and approximately half of them also have learning disabilities such as dyslexia.

The hallmarks of ADHD are inattention, talking a lot, inability to take instruction, frequently calling out in class, doing dangerous or impulsive things, acting before they think, being easily upset or easily angered (explosive temper), and struggling to make and keep friends.

The question is, are children much more hyperactive today than they were in the past, or have our lifestyles changed so fundamentally that children just appear to be hyperactive?

Well, the jury is still out. But we think the condition is over-diagnosed and that way too many Kiwi kids are being unnecessarily medicated instead of parents, teachers and medical professionals exploring why so many boys are labelled ADHD and finding more creative ways to deal with their high energy levels.

Unfortunately, the condition is often diagnosed by a general practitioner and is usually treated—somewhat ironically—with stimulants such as Ritalin, Adderall and Vyvanse that both increase blood flow and the levels of certain chemicals in the brain, such as dopamine and norepinephrine, which help transmit signals between nerves. The theory is that kids with ADHD are constantly self-stimulating in an effort to produce these effects and these medications do that work for them, allowing messages to get through more easily. Proponents say they have a long safety record, they take effect within minutes and leave the body within hours, and are not addictive in the doses prescribed for ADHD. But they do come with side-effects, and clinical studies are now linking adult drug addiction with adolescents who have been prescribed Ritalin.

The New Zealand ADHD Association says deciding whether someone has ADHD requires careful assessment and determination by a specialist, usually a paediatrician or psychiatrist. According to its website, 'The diagnosis is based on extensive data of developmental, learning, social and behavioural areas, drawn from a range of sources. The parent's input is critical for an accurate diagnosis.'

We agree. Over the last 10 years we've seen a big rise in the number of boys coming onto the Big Buddy programme who have been diagnosed with ADHD. We're not black and white on this issue but what we do see is an over-diagnosis: any boy who is very active seems to be labelled ADHD. We're also not saying ADHD doesn't exist, but we believe it's a clinical condition that is quite difficult to diagnose and we don't think GPs should be diagnosing or prescribing for it. However, there is certainly a need for medication in those extreme cases where boys are jumping off the walls and unable to fulfil their potential because of ADHD.

We believe it's also helpful to address the causes of ADHD, such as:

- Sedentary lifestyles, in which kids watch far too much TV and spend hours on media devices, affecting their ability to self-stimulate.
- A risk-adverse approach to play—the 'cotton-wooling' of children.
- Diet—with sugar and preservatives singled out as the worst contributors to behavioural issues.
- School environments unsuited to boys' learning modalities, i.e. not active enough, aural rather than kinaesthetic learning.
- A lack of male teachers in schools, who bring a different approach to teaching, providing more focused learning in shorter bursts.

These ideas are supported by science writer Richard DeGrandpre, who questioned the link between exposure to technology, particularly television, and ADD (the precursor diagnosis to ADHD) in his ground-breaking book *Ritalin Nation*, published in 2000. 'With there being so many sources for obtaining effortless stimulation, and with the stimuli intensifying, we have to wonder not only about what we are spending our time doing but also about what we are doing no longer,' he writes.

He talks about us living in a 'rapid-fire culture' and the importance of keeping 'accelerated moments in check by taking pockets of slowness'.

The late Bruce Mackie, a neuro-feedback pioneer and director of the Lifeline counselling service, also supported this theory, saying boys with ADHD were losing the ability to internally stimulate because it was all being done from the outside. 'They are no longer stimulating their brains through the imagination, playing, fighting, debates and conversation. Once they've lost that ability, they become addicted to external stimulation,' Mackie told Richard during a number of discussions on this subject.

In place of stimulant medications, Mackie used neuro-feedback or 'brain training' to teach kids to self-stimulate—he literally hyped them up internally, so they didn't need external stimulants.

Big Buddy programme manager Steve Sobota, who has worked with dozens of boys diagnosed with ADHD, sees four important areas: 'Diagnosis—who's making it and why; schooling—the lack of male teachers and classroom structure; diet—sugar is a big one for me but also preservatives, colourings, etc.—and lack of physical exercise—both at school and outside of it; and parenting styles—lack of consistent, meaningful boundaries, etc.

'I think my schooling was pretty similar [to today], with lots of desk-based learning, but I think the thing that has changed most is the lack of male teachers in primary schools. I think as teachers, they probably do things differently. My boy has just started school and I'm really interested in how that is going to work out. At the moment there are three male teachers in a school of 700 pupils. I'm keen for him to have a male teacher but that doesn't mean you don't have to check out what sort of teacher that male teacher is.'

Sobota says boys also need a lot more exposure to nature. 'I think it's a strong urge for boys and men. It could be something to do with why boys are over-diagnosed with this or that disorder. They need more time in nature—connecting to the earth and themselves. A bit more quiet time would balance their busy, stressful lives; city, school, home, etc. It's a way of coming home to yourself and boys and men do this easily.

'As an example, one of our mentors is really into hunting. I asked him if he liked killing things and he said he didn't really care if he didn't catch anything; he just liked taking his rifle and going up into the bush, having time and space and peace—and not talking to anyone. That's more what he got from it. I found it really fascinating.

'Guys who are into fishing say the same thing; it's not so much about catching fish as just sitting out there in nature and contemplating the world.'

So, our advice is to get your boys outside doing stuff in the world that stimulates their bodies, minds, senses and imaginations. Shut down the technology and go fly a kite, make a go-cart, jump off a wharf . . . just do it! Try to make sure busy boys have a male teacher, cut the junk out of their diets and make sure your boundaries are consistent and fair. If hyperactivity is still limiting your boy's ability to play, learn and socialise, then get help.

Busy boy advice

- Make sure your boy is very physically active—get them out in nature and reduce all screen time.
- Examine his diet—heavily reduce sugar, preservatives and colourings.
- Do a 360 degree review of him—at home, at school, his socialisation.
- See if it's possible to get him into a class with a male teacher.
- Check out boy-friendly schools in your area.
- Make sure you have clear everyday routines at home.
- Make reminder lists together if it helps him to remember tasks.
- Set consistent, meaningful boundaries.
- Encourage your child to talk and make sure you *listen.*
- Build on your boy's strengths.
- If you are still worried, ask your doctor for a referral to a paediatrician.
- Research current info on ADHD medications.
- Try alternative therapies (possibly in conjunction with medication).

Don't slag off his dad/mum

If you're separated or divorced from your boy's dad, don't slag him off in front of your boy. Save that for your friends! Because no matter what kind of arsehole you think your ex is, he's still your boy's father and your son identifies with him as male. Unless he was abusive to the point where contact with your son is dangerous, the chances are they going to have some sort of relationship with each other.

As a mother, you hopefully saw something good in your ex when you conceived a child with him (excluding rape conceptions, of course) and it's important that you dig deep into those memories and try to find some generosity towards him—for your boy's sake. Remember, *he's* not divorced from his father—you are. He might have been a lousy partner and in your opinion a waste-of-space father but the truth is, your boy is still going to look to him for fathering and masculine affirmation—something you cannot give him.

Somewhere deep in every boy's psyche sits his dad. Good dad, bad dad—doesn't matter; he still sits there. To slag off that father is to slag off that part in your boy. Inside, he suspects he will inherit something of his father, so hearing someone he respects say his father was bad to the bone will cause him an impossible internal struggle. It won't be until your boy is much older that he can look at his dad—and the ghost of his dad inside himself—with any reason and reflection.

Similarly, for the separated/divorced blokes—don't slag off your son's mum in front of him. He loves her and she's a touchstone for him—ask yourself if you'd want your security ripped out from under you. You felt something for this woman once. Respect is the key here—honour the fact that you had a kid together and you both owe that kid a decent life.

This golden rule also applies when parents are still together—it will not work for any of you long term if you run down the other parent to your boy. Don't ask him to collude with you against your partner—he needs to love you both. If you've got issues with your mate, don't involve your son in them. He cannot and should not have to choose between you, and he is way too young to be involved in your adult relationship. Talk to your friends or a counsellor—that'll leave you freed up to have the parent-child relationship with your boy that he needs to grow into a healthy man. Hell, growing up is complex enough without carrying around the unprocessed baggage of your parents' issues as well!

Step-parenting

Step-parenting is where the proverbial rubber hits the road when it comes to parenting. It's the hardest gig of all. Parents meet, they fall in love and bam . . . welcome to instant family! But *The Brady Bunch* it ain't.

Despite the best intentions of loved-up parents to create the perfect blended family, the challenges are enormous, as the children adjust to having new step-parents and step-siblings. Kids don't know how these changes will affect their relationships with their own parents and natural siblings, if they have them. 'Will Dad still love me as much if that boy is living with him?' 'Will I see him as much?' 'I don't like the food she cooks—it's different to Mum's.' 'I don't want to share a bedroom with someone.' The questions and challenges are complicated and mind-bending.

All the advice is to take it slowly and think through very carefully how you want your new blended family to function—give everyone time to adjust and get to know each other; to sort out the pecking order and adjust according to their age and stage.

We need to say here that we got a lot wrong when we fell in love in 1983 and set about 'blending' our two families. We dived in too quickly; lived together and married too soon; had way too many expectations of our kids 'blending' into the harmonious family we imagined as the oxytocin surged hot in our veins. We didn't give our three kids (then aged three, four and eight) time to adjust and get to know each other—hell, they were still reeling from the recent separation of their biological parents, let alone being expected to transition into a new family. We simply didn't think through the relationships enough. Mainly, and this is painful to admit, we thought more about ourselves and our needs than we did about what our kids needed. It's something we sorely regret and would do differently in hindsight.

Fortunately, there's a lot more information and advice available now on how to do it better, and we recommend you tap into it in the very early stages of forming any new relationship. Some things to think about if you are a new blended family include:

- **Children get unsettled by having too many changes at once.** Take it slowly—blended families are much more likely to succeed if couples wait two years after divorce to remarry.
- **Don't expect to love your partner's children overnight—or them you.** You'll need to get know each other, which takes time.
- **Do ordinary, everyday stuff together as a family.** Don't make you all being together a big deal, involving expensive outings, etc. You can't buy love and connection. Cook together, mow lawns—do what other families do.
- **Discuss your parenting styles and make some agreements on how you are going to do this together.** You'll need to decide who is disciplining who and how. It's the area most step-parents come unstuck on.

- **Don't allow ultimatums.** Your kids or new partner may put you in uncomfortable situations where you feel you have to choose between them. Tell them that you want *both* of them in your life and that you're all going to have to find ways to get along.
- **Insist on respect.** You can't insist people like each other but you can insist that they treat one another with respect.

Given time and the right support, kids should gradually adjust to their step-parents and to being part of a new family. It is your job to communicate clearly, openly and sensitively, and meet their needs for security, to give them the best shot at a successful transition. Good luck!

And don't despair—despite getting so much wrong when we blended our families, today we are a close, motley crew who love, support and have each other's backs. We went through some pretty raging fires to get to this place and sometimes the ashes of those fires can flare, but we largely function well—either talking things through or giving each other space to lick wounds when necessary. It's never long before we all remember our strong commitment to family and come back together. We are very grateful for this grace. So take heart . . . if you don't get it all right (and you won't), there's still hope!

Summary

What a mission! We've explored all sorts of themes and your boy is still only seven! Oh well, onwards—we've got many years to enjoy yet as he continues his road to manhood. Here's a wrap up of what we've covered in *Stepping out: 4 to 7 years*:

- Your son's cognitive abilities are on the rise as his frontal cortex slowly controls more of his learning.
- He may or may not have a testosterone surge at the age of four.
- He's slowly moving away from his mother—she needs to step back and 'trust' more.
- It's time for Dad to step forward and welcome his boy to the tribe.
- You're learning on the job.
- You need to be authentic.
- Boys have good bullshit detectors.
- Men and women parent differently.
- You need to explore and understand your own emotional drivers.
- There might be some sibling stuff going down.
- Eat the same food at the same time if you can.
- Knock bullying on the head.
- Weapons play is OK.
- Introduce your boy to his ancestors.
- He's looking for heroes to emulate.
- Authentic praise is like gold to your boy.
- Think hard about whether your boy is ready for school at five.
- Let who your boy is be your guide when choosing a primary school.
- ADHD is a minefield that requires very careful diagnosis and treatment.
- Don't slag off his mum/dad—whether you are together or separated.
- Blending step-families takes time.

We think the take-away message from this chapter is that maleness is caught—not taught. Your boy is going to become a man through observing the men around him, so the better quality of blokes he has in his life, the richer he'll be.

How you are in the world will make a power of difference to him as he nudges up against and absorbs qualities from his peers at school. Fathers—be the man you want your boy to become. Mothers—support your partner to be the best man he can be. And give him some rope as he leans into fathering—he's learning on the job and will be a better man for having done so.

Activity suggestions for younger boys

- Teach your boy how to light a fire.
- Teach him how to throw a spear.
- Start a garden; learn about the care of soil and plants and the use of tools.
- Go to your local library; help your boy get a library card.
- Visit the tallest building you can find and go up and down the escalators.
- Go ice skating, roller skating or rollerblading.
- Wash a car together.
- Watch a parade.
- Go to the beach, play ball, take the dog for a walk, race up and slide down sand dunes.
- Go swimming.
- Attend a dog show.
- Find a court for basketball practice, or a field for rugby/ soccer practice.

- Visit a museum.
- Go for a bushwalk.
- Go to the park, take chess or a chequers board, maybe fly a kite.
- Attend a play.
- Play miniature golf.
- Visit the fire station or police station on their open days.
- Pick fruit together: apples, strawberries, etc.
- Make lunch and go on a picnic.
- Read a book together.
- Go to car-sales yard and take a new car for test drive.
- Get torches and discover local tunnels.
- Use cardboard to slide down the sides of hills and sand dunes.
- Visit a local naval base.
- Go to the observatory; check out the stars and planets.
- Go fishing off a wharf.
- Go to some of the free music events in your town/city.
- Rotate the tyres on your car or change the oil together.
- Go bike riding in a park.
- Put up a tent.
- Get creative with some timber and a hammer and nails.
- Play sports or discuss your favourites.
- Draw chalk pictures on concrete.
- Buy a yo-yo and learn how to do tricks with it.
- Buy a hacky-sack and learn how to use it.
- Enjoy a fresh coconut or pineapple.

- Egg drop—make a container that will keep an egg from breaking when dropped from a height.
- Make a scrapbook of all the things you do together. Include things like stories, pictures, song lyrics and other mementos.
- Play fight.
- Pull apart clocks and machines.
- Dig holes and sit in them.

THREE

The explorer: 8 to 11 years

My father didn't tell me how to live; he lived, and let me watch him do it.

Clarence Budington Kelland

These are golden years. There's a naïve inquisitiveness to boys this age that is very endearing—well, most of the time anyway! They are interested in how everything works and will drive you crazy with thousands of questions, but the upside is they find the fun in everything; they'll show you a good time if you roll with their quirky interests.

Your 'tween' (as J.R.R. Tolkien famously coined the late-maturing Hobbits in *The Lord of the Rings*) is about to go through some big growth developments that will broaden his world and make life more interesting, as his cognitive and physical abilities go ahead in leaps and bounds and you are able to do lots more stuff together. Here's a bit of a steer on the changes he'll go through.

Your boy will gain 2 to 3 kilograms a year on average during this period as he continues to build muscle mass and improve both his gross- and fine-motor skills. This is interesting to watch, as he gains more control over his body and has better coordination to carry out the whole-body movements needed in sporting activities like throwing a rugby ball, dribbling a basketball or batting. Now that his gross motor, cognitive and social skills are maturing, he's also becoming a capable and competitive sports-team member (if that's his bag).

By now his permanent adult teeth are starting to push through the gums, loosening and replacing his baby teeth. He'll have lost his front teeth when he was about six and be growing new ones sometime about now, but the molars (back teeth) won't loosen until he's about 10 to 12.

During middle childhood, your boy's bones will broaden and lengthen dramatically. He'll grow an average of 5 to 7.5 centimetres every year; he'll be taller than most girls at the beginning of this period but likely shorter than them by the end of it—something he may struggle with as his adolescent hormones begin kicking in and he desperately wants to be attractive to girls, if that's his orientation.

Sometimes, boys of this age will complain about pain in their arms and legs—caused by bone growth outpacing the growth of surrounding muscles and tendons. Up to 40 per cent of kids complain about 'growing pains' between to ages of 8 and 12, according to the American Academy of Paediatrics, but they're generally nothing to worry about. Hot-water bottles or wheat bags, light massage and warm baths should relieve the pain—but if they start really affecting your boy's life, then see a doctor for more advice.

His fine-motor skill development—requiring hand-eye coordination—will also increase rapidly over this period. Your boy will be able to write and draw better, with his drawings becoming more complex as he incorporates depth and three-dimensional elements into his work. Watching his fine-motor skills combine with his vivid imagination will be a joy to watch as he produces ever more complex drawings. He'll also be much more able to tackle detail-oriented craft projects like building models, and he'll be able to start using simple tools like a hammer or drill (under supervision, of course) or a hand mixer as he's whipping up a storm in the kitchen.

So now is a really good time to start making and doing lots of stuff with your boy. He'll love coming up with ideas with you and planning out how to achieve them—just be aware that he may have a tendency towards being forgetful and disorganised, so plans may need a lot of 'along-siding' from you to come to fruition and give him the sense of mastery and accomplishment that will grow him well.

Along with all this activity, now is also a good time to help your boy safely explore risk and/or danger. Unfortunately—or fortunately—not everything he wants to do will be nice and safe. (See 'Bumps and bruises' on page 33.) Remember your boy needs to experience manageable risks at this age, so he has at least some background to risk-taking when he becomes a young man and you are not alongside him.

But one word of warning—as your boy's hand-eye coordination skills improve, he's also likely to start beating you at online games, so best be practising your 'good loser' behaviour! Remember, he's modelling off your responses, and being a bad loser is not a good look.

Also be aware that your son is going to ask you *lots* of questions, and some of them are going to challenge you. Everything from 'Why aren't birds electrocuted when they stand on power lines?' to 'What is time?' to 'Why is that man homeless?' to 'Why do people get sick?'

and the kicker, 'Why was Mum yelling out last night?' We figure if he's old enough to ask a question, he should always get a true answer based on his age level and ability to understand.

For example, many scientists would say 'time' is the flow of cause and effect—that according to Einstein's theory of general relativity, time is the path which an object will take through a four-dimensional universe when left to itself. But would you say this to your nine-year-old? No. Maybe try: 'Everything is always getting older—the grass is getting older, the cheese in the fridge is getting older, the table in this room is getting older, and people and animals are always getting older, too. Time is a way of measuring things getting older, a way of helping us to see exactly how much older anything is getting.'

Or when he asks why birds don't get electrocuted on power lines, you wouldn't tell him, 'For a bird to be electrocuted it would need to touch two wires at different voltages, or one wire and the grounded structure of the pylon, at the same time. If they did this there would be a current flow and the bird would be likely to be electrocuted.' No. How about: 'Because the wires are only dangerous when there is a way to touch the ground. If the birds had one foot on the wire and one on the ground, they would be electrocuted.'

Trickier, we grant you, are the 'Why was Mum yelling out last night?' questions, but you'll just have to wing it with something like, 'Look, I know this sounds gross to you now, but trust me, it will seem different when you're older. Mum and I were having sex—you know, when a man's penis goes inside a woman's vagina and sometimes babies are made. Well, we were doing that and Mum got a bit excited and called out. That's all it was.' You know your son best and will be able to gauge what he is capable of understanding. (See 'Let's talk about sex' on page 129.)

Our biggest blooper in this department was when our 11-year-old caught us out on the lounge floor late one night. In response to her asking what we were doing, red-faced father said: 'Naked wrestling.' That story lives on in family lore—sex now being referred to as naked wrestling! We continue to contribute to their therapy costs!

So your boy is developing quickly, has much better cognitive, motor and social skills, and is asking some hard questions. But let's face it—eight-year-old boys are still predominantly focused on their own needs. It will require a leap of faith to believe they can move from 'What's in this for me?' to developing a conscience around the concept of fairness, e.g. 'If you do this for me, I'll do this for you.' What's on your side is that gaining social approval and living up to the expectations of people close to them is becoming increasingly important to tweens. A major emotional step for boys of this age group is the realisation that self-interest may need to take a back seat to the needs of others. Another giant step for boykind!

From here on in, your boy's self-concept is going to be increasingly influenced by his peers. Although 8- to 11-year-old boys generally have a low level of concern about their physical appearance, this will be influenced by his peers as well as the media. Sadly, it's when many boys experience strong pressure to conform to 'masculine' stereotypes and can go underground with their emergent sexuality as they strive to conform to 'norms'. (See 'Finding his sexual compass' on page 172.)

Tweens can also be filled with anxiety. American Academy of Paediatrics fellow Dr John Mersch says on MedicineNet.com that the development of real fears—such as kidnappings, war and violence—replaces fantasy fears—such as witches, monsters and the bogeyman during these years. Dr Mersch believes this is related to the development of the concept of delayed gratification, as kids learn that what they do now can impact on the future.

These middle years are a journey onto the path of self-identity, independence and development of moral values. Your boy is on his way to becoming a young man.

During this time he'll likely experience his first 'puppy love'—where his infatuation moves from you—his parents—to someone else. Be prepared for a rocky ride, folks—his heart will be broken and once again, you'll agonise for him, but make this journey he must. Your job now is to stand alongside him—loving him when he hates himself—rekindling his hope and encouraging him to keep walking into his brilliant future. You're moving from caretaker to cheerleader.

Six dangerous things your kids should do

1. Play with fire.
2. Own a pocket knife (first universal tool—empowering).
3. Throw a spear (stimulates and strengthens the frontal lobes).
4. Deconstruct appliances (gives a sense that the world is 'knowable').
5. Break online media copyright laws (learn how laws can be inadvertently broken).
6. Drive a car—in a safe environment (gives kids a handle on the world—that they can have control).

Gever Tulley, writer and founder of the Tinkering School

He's pushing back

Setting boundaries is going to get tougher from now on as you learn to negotiate, rather than dictate—not necessarily an easy transition for some of us!

Whereas once you could get away with 'Because I said so', now you're going to have to try something like, 'This is what I'd like to do—what do you think about that?'

From about the age of nine onwards, boys start inhabiting their bodies more and have opinions and ideas about what they like and want to do, says Big Buddy programme manager Steve Sobota. 'They want to take more ownership around what they do—they want a say.'

It's certainly around this age that we start getting calls at Big Buddy from mothers and caregivers saying their previously compliant son is 'answering back'; 'becoming defiant' and 'is difficult'. He may be starting to get into a bit of trouble at school as he explores his place in the social order of things within his peer group and asks himself: 'Where do I fit in?' and 'Who is my tribe?'. He may well be much more interested in his social connections than he is in you right now.

Try not to be hurt by this seeming shift in loyalties; what's actually happening here is he's getting ready to 'cross the bridge' into manhood, which usually happens from about the age of 11, according to author and social commentator Celia Lashlie (1953–2015), who penned the bestselling book on raising boys *He'll Be OK: Growing Gorgeous Boys into Good Men*. To do this, your boy needs to gradually separate from you for a time. Trust that he will come back. Your choice is either to try to stop him getting onto the bridge or help him across it—and you know what the right decision is here, people!

Lashlie described these early steps onto the 'bridge of adolescence' as being a time for mothers to begin stepping back and for fathers—if they are around—to 'make themselves clearly visible at the edge of the bridge so they can be seen by both their sons and their wives or partners, and so there is plenty of time for all involved to adjust to the impending change'.

Mothers will need to pull back from the level of direct involvement with their sons in order to ease their transition to manhood, Lashlie wrote.

However, if there isn't a man around who mothers can trust will care for their sons as they walk the bridge, Lashlie was clear that mothers should do it, and not abandon their boys. Great advice from that wise woman.

Painful as separation from their boys may be for mothers, our experience is that big issues arise if that split doesn't happen. When we interview men to be volunteer mentors, we can see the ones who haven't done it—they're still looking after their mothers 40 years later, and resent the hell out of them! It seems to change their relationships with women. If we get a strong 'hooky mother' story, we are really careful about who we match the guy with—not so much about the boy we match him up with, but about the boy's mother. Because if the man hasn't formed his own masculine identity as separate to his mother, *all* women will be 'mother' to him (hey, you women know about this!).

Our advice to mothers during this time is not to take it personally when you get push-back from your son. It's not revenge and it's not your fault. Trust that the relationship you've established over the last 11 or so years will see you right—the foundations are in place. Let your boy do the pushing and come up with creative ideas about how to roll with him; maybe think about doing some physical stuff together like climbing mountains, training for fun runs or bike riding. Find something he likes and encourage him to get into it; it will provide an anchor in his life as he walks the bridge.

Sometimes we see mums sort of drift along and fly out with their boys—moving from one interest to the next in quick succession in the desperate hope of getting their boy back on track (and avoiding the bridge). But if you encourage him to stick with an activity—unless he really hates it, of course—it will be better in the long term; he'll learn resilience through working his way through the hard stuff and feel a sense of achievement and accomplishment.

Find your full stop

Clinical psychologist and parenting guru Nigel Latta's advice to parents—particularly mothers—when it comes to setting boundaries with boy tweens cannot be bettered: 'Be brief,' Latta said in a *New Zealand Herald* article. 'Say what you need to say then shut up: "No, you can't go to your friend's place tonight. Full stop."; "I want you to tidy up your room now. Full stop."'

Unfortunately, we women tend to bang on a bit when short and sweet will do the business. All our boy hears when we bang on is 'Blah, blah, blah . . .'. He's over it!

Boys' brains are simple. They respond to instruction and boundaries really well, as long as they are clearly articulated. They don't do well with emotional content, so when we're advising our mentors we say, 'Have no emotion in your voice whatsoever—just lower your voice and say, "Don't eat food like that at my table. Full stop."' When mothers say, 'Look how you're eating your food . . . you eat like a pig . . . what about all the starving kids in Africa?' the boy's thinking, 'What the f . . . have they got to do with it?' and the original message gets completely lost. The old 'less is more' will get better results.

Latta also advises parents against making their kids' problems their own. For example, if his room's a pigsty and you want it cleaned up, instead of saying, 'Why should the rest of us have to live in a house that stinks because you're too lazy to clean up your room?', he advises you say, 'You have one hour to clean up your room. If you don't, I will be coming in with a large plastic bag and throwing anything I think is suspect into that bag and taking it to the dump. Your time starts now.'

The important thing is to have realistic expectations—you have a right to demand a reasonably tidy, vermin-free bedroom but not an immaculately clean one.

It's also really important that parents, particularly mothers, don't shame their boys when they set boundaries or discipline them. Boys have a hyper-sensitivity to shame, particularly from a woman—it's toxic to them and can affect them for the rest of their lives. If it's shaming by Mum, it will affect their relationships with women as they get older. Shaming by Dad will affect their relationships with men and authority figures when older.

Simply put, shaming happens when you criticise or say 'no' to the person, rather than to their behaviour, e.g. 'You are lazy/dumb/ ignorant . . .'; 'You are a bad boy/lazy boy/smelly boy . . .' Not helpful—and it won't work to modify the behaviour.

Shaming him won't make one blind bit of different to the outcome you want, e.g. a tidy room, less noise, etc. Straight-forward, crisp statements à la Nigel Latta will produce a much better outcome. Granted, *you* may feel better having blown off some steam by shaming him, but it will only create bigger problems for yourself and your boy down the track.

Remember, *we* are the parents here, *we* hold the wider, longer-term view and it's our task to vent our frustration somewhere else, with someone else, some other way—*not* to dump it on our boy. Yes, we agree there will be times when 'lazy, dirty pig' may be a perfectly accurate description of your boy, but all he will do is add it to his little bag of shame that he carries into his future. And his room will still be a pigsty!

Latta told the *New Zealand Herald* that establishing a one-on-one relationship with your teenager is vital to good parenting: 'All discipline systems are built on a bedrock of relationship. Without it, you have no leverage. And this is not a friendship: Your kid has plenty of friends. He needs parents.'

Dr Mark Bowers, author of *8 Keys to Raising the Quirky Child: How to Help a Kid Who Doesn't (Quite) Fit In*, told Radio New Zealand National that it's crucial to wait for 'parenting moments' to talk through issues. 'Because insight and self-awareness might not peak until 9 to 12, you have to wait till they are in a good mood and calm, and not doing the behaviour—you have to wait for those moments to get through to them.'

Long-time teacher Del McFarlane-Scott says being honest with boys is what establishes trust. 'Boys are black and white. They need you to tell it like it is.

'If I've got a boy in trouble, I use a restorative justice process involving a piece of rope. I take the piece of rope and say, "At the moment the problem is this size (small). And we need to sort it out." Every time they tell me something that doesn't feel honest, I make the rope a bit longer—explain to them that the problem is getting bigger.

'I'm not telling them to stop telling lies—they see a physical thing that tells them the problem is growing. Then I say, "When you're ready we can start reducing this." Every boy I've ever done this with gets it! They are controlling it—they are making choices. As they start 'fessing up the rope gets smaller and we start fixing the problem.' Result!

Finding an interest

As Mum steps back, Dad (or a good bloke you know) is hopefully stepping forward, providing a much-needed anchor as boys embark on this interesting but fraught journey to manhood. They are ready for lots more exploring and stretching their environmental parameters, so get your thinking cap on and start brainstorming ways to encourage and inspire your boy to try new things. (See 'Excellent activities for older boys' on page 136.)

One way men can do this is simply by being themselves and letting their boys come along for the ride. Get your boy alongside you doing the sort of male exploring and creating you like to do, for example, climbing big hills, trees and walls; fishing, tramping and camping; lighting fires; painting sheds and doing stuff in sheds; building stuff; putting tents up (really efficiently and fast!); rope work (tying cool and useful knots); playing games; looking at art (and making it); the hushed awe of admiring a really great bridge, truck, tractor or machine.

The other important way to encourage your boy is through noticing what's emerging in him—glimpsing what interests or fascinates him and then taking one of these interests and helping your boy explore it fully. An eight-year-old boy will not know what he is capable of but when you help guide him along the lines of an interest towards fully experiencing it, you have taught him the all-important gift of 'manifesting'—of 'making it so'—something men are really good at.

For example, say your boy starts showing an interest in drawing. You draw with him; you get him good-quality pencils, paints, charcoal, etc., and explore the different media to draw with. You do some guerrilla drawing—chalk on footpaths; you take him to an art gallery; you take him along to meet a real artist. Take it one step at a time and when the interest wanes, don't keep pushing—wait to glimpse the next interest and roll with that. The key is being alongside him as he explores and develops his interests.

By your actions you are teaching him the importance of curiosity and developing his confidence to try new stuff. 'Hell, I don't know much about that but it looks really interesting—let's get stuck in and figure it out.' That's what he needs from you.

It's all about the relationship

The relationship you have with your boy is so much about time— regular time, a rhythm of engagement that tells your boy he's important to you, not just now and then, but time after time, week after week, year after year.

Every relationship is different and it takes time to see how they work. Even if it's your own son and you've established a bond from birth, relationships still need energy and review to make sure they remain healthy. Be prepared to look at him with new eyes as he grows and ask yourself if what you've always done is still working for both of you. Does he need more physical or mental stimulation? Different discussions from what you've previously had? New challenges?

Do you need to shake up your timetable to allow more time with him? Make a regular weekend date?

In our experience, regular and real time spent together pays off more than big flashy experiences, although these peak events do have their place, like when a father or mentor takes a boy to see a big male hero and is there afterwards to help him integrate the experience. For example, after going to the All Blacks Rugby World Cup parade together, you could talk about what it is that you both admire in men like Dan Carter and Richie McCaw. Is it their skill? Team spirit? Determination? Perseverance against the odds? These events provide perfect opportunities to discuss values and traits—for you and your boy to explore admiration versus adoration and what makes a good man.

At Big Buddy our model is 'relational'—following the relationship—rather than about 'doing', although boys, particularly, like to do! It's not about coaching or setting goals. It's less achievement-focused and more about veneration—particularly in relation to men, because we believe boys learn to be men through venerating other men. It's really about just hanging out together doing ordinary things and seeing what happens from that—what ideas bubble up in the course of doing ordinary stuff that ignites his interest that you can follow up on.

Quality of time is key

We need to stress here it's not about the *amount* of time you spend with your boy—it's about the *quality* of it. It doesn't take much: turn off your devices and be really present with your boy. Our Big Buddy mentors spend around one afternoon a week with their Little Buddies, and even this brief exposure can have a huge impact. Mothers report boys hanging out for the weekend when their mentor will come to pick them up—they wait at the gate. And it's about doing simple things together.

Quality is about 'being' as much as 'doing'. Boys seeing how men do stuff, and often the being-ness of maleness is experienced through doing. For example, one of our mentors decided to just change the oil in his car with his Little Buddy one Saturday. Well . . . according to the boy's mother, it was the best day of her son's life! She'd never seen him so excited when he came home.

From now on your boy will need very regular, quality time with a good man—preferably his father—at least once a week; dedicated time, in our experience. He'll be pretty enthusiastic about doing all sorts of diverse activities—just keep rolling out ideas and respond to his suggestions. This is the age of exploration for you and your boy—but remember, it won't last forever.

From the age of about 14 upwards, the contact will need to be much more sensitive to the boy, taking account of his own peer, sporting and cultural interests. For example, if he's practising with his school band on Saturday afternoon, hanging out with his friends in the evening and playing soccer on Sunday, it may be that you organise to go for a pizza on Sunday evening—just a couple of easy hours catching up on where he's at. It will change from him fitting into your busy schedule to you fitting into his!

Respecting silence

The key to good parenting is communication. And that doesn't mean you always have to talk—just hanging out together, doing ordinary things, will be enough to establish good relationships.

Respecting silence is a really critical part of parenting boys—they do well with it. We think men, and New Zealand men in particular, have a special relationship with holding silence, and it is a valuable experience that grows boys into men. Men usually do silence when focusing on doing or seeing. Fishing is classic—long silent moments staring hopefully at the water: 'Shh . . . you'll scare the fish away.' Walking or tramping in the bush: 'Shh . . . you'll scare the birds.' Silently staring at the fire you just built. Simply nodding when another man speaks. Shaking hands in silence.

Knowing when to hold your tongue is a great discipline for a boy to learn. Hey, we all remember those times when we wished we'd held our tongue! In a busy, noisy world, a man who can hold silence appropriately (a key word, because speaking is good too!) also holds respect.

Field of fathering

At Big Buddy we talk about a 'field of fathering', because we believe it's important to have a mix of men in boys' lives—birth fathers, stepfathers, grandfathers, uncles and mentors. The more male mentors in a boy's life the better, we reckon!

These mentors will hopefully continue throughout your boy's life in the form of teachers, coaches, bosses, community leaders, etc. They can even come from unexpected places, in unusual ways.

For example, our son-in-law befriended an old man who lives in a state house—threatened with demolition to make way for a housing development—in a wealthy suburb down the road from him. This old boy, who has no family other than an older brother who he doesn't have a lot of contact with, started out by mowing our daughter and son-in-law's lawn. When he got past being able to do that, our son-in-law kept visiting him and now takes him to hospital when he needs to go, takes his kids to visit the old boy and his chickens, and gets great gardening advice from him. Caring for this old guy in between juggling an already busy life with a full-time job and a family has engendered compassion and caring in our son-in-law, which is lovely to see. Mentors are not always about goals and achievement—they can work much more subtly on developing our moral character.

Despite the African proverb 'It takes a village to raise a child' being bandied about, the truth is we mostly live in small, isolated family cohorts that are a far cry from the whole tribe being involved in raising children. Mum, Dad and two kids doth not maketh a tribe! Usually, in European families anyway, the village may extend to grandparents, aunts and uncles and a few cousins, if your kid is lucky. Hey, you may even know and have time to have relationships with a few of your neighbours! But even that is getting diluted as populations shift in a shrinking global market and people migrate for jobs or lifestyle, intermarry, etc. It's getting harder to find—and keep—your tribe, which does have implications for how we raise our kids.

Our choices are either to prioritise the importance of kids' cultural connections to family and friends or to trust they will maintain relationships, regardless of distance and culture. Fortunately, we have fantastic tools like Skype to help us stay connected, and these are very valid and useful ways to stay in touch with loved ones. Our sister-in-law had a weekly Skype date with her small granddaughter living overseas (interspersed with in-person visits) for nearly four years. During these online visits, she read bedtime stories to her beloved grandchild and was able to virtually 'kiss' her goodnight. It worked well, and now that her grandchild is living back here in New Zealand, they are very well bonded as a result of this regular online contact.

Another good example of digital bonding is when one of our Big Buddy mentors got a job overseas, he kept regular contact with his Little Buddy via Skype for a couple of years until that boy was old enough to travel overseas to see his mentor. The bond they'd established was seamlessly continued.

Small amounts of contact time can make a huge difference and anyone can get in on that act via social media. Indeed, we can 'create a village'—it just takes effort to bed in the contact.

Closer to home, it's a matter of finding good men who are happy to be involved in your boy's life. We find one visit a month from an uncle, for example, can make a huge difference—he smells different, speaks differently to your boy's immediate family. He'll have different interests and be able to expand your boy's experience in ways you might not have imagined. Boys need to know there are different types of people in the world as they slowly develop, and we encourage mothers to find those men in their communities for their sons. (See 'Father hunger' on page 50.)

Beyond sport

It's also good for boys to be exposed to more than sport. There's not a lot of exposure to literature and art compared to sport for boys, and that's sad. People tend to stereotype boys as needing lots of action, which is true, but they are more than action.

We had a Samoan mentor, who owned a kick-boxing gym, matched with a boy who was also into kick-boxing—he had posters all over his bedroom walls of kick-boxers. Choice, we thought—that's an easy match. But when it came to their first outing they went and played chess in the Auckland Domain! The guy said he wanted to explore something other than his day job and his Little Buddy was up for that too.

So, boys need exposure to a wide range of what's available. Sport needs to be balanced with arts and crafts for creative expression. And it's not always true that physical sports enable boys to 'get it out of their systems'—they can also encourage more aggression if not balanced with other forms of expression, so think outside the box when you're scanning for potential mentors and activities.

Many of the men we've interviewed talked about feeling very grateful for the diverse mentors in their lives—particularly fathers, grandfathers, uncles and significant male bosses who have given them something to aspire to—an image of manhood worthy of striving for. You can't underestimate the power of that.

Safety around other men

It's about now your boy starts wanting to go out into the world more, and with that comes risk. He's exploring—checking out different activities and hobbies. In the course of doing so, he's going to come into contact with people you don't know—teachers, coaches, other kids' parents, etc.

Most importantly, he's going to meet men you don't know. You may worry that one of them is going to be a paedophile who will exploit your boy. That's every parent's fear, so we may as well get it out there. The reality is there are sexual predators who groom and abuse young boys, and it scars those young men for life.

As CEO of Big Buddy, it's the thing that kept me (Richard) awake at night when I first took over an organisation that matched volunteer male mentors with fatherless boys. I knew they would often be alone together and that the mothers entrusting their boys into our care needed to know they were safe. So that was the commitment I made to myself—if I was going to do this, I would make sure I had done everything humanly possible to make sure the boys in our care were safe.

I started by reviewing all the available research on paedophiles and talked extensively with psychologists worldwide to see if it was possible to detect sexual predators before they committed abuse. I discovered it was possible (not 100 per cent—nothing ever is) but that through in-depth interviewing and taking a 360-degree look at a person, you can reasonably accurately predict sexual behaviour. On the back of that research we developed the world-renowned Big Buddy screening process, and I am proud to say we have not had an allegation of abuse in the 13-plus years I been with Big Buddy.

So how does it work? We look at a picture of health, rather than of dysfunction. The psychological model generally looks at what's wrong with a person, whereas we use the psychotherapeutic model to look at strengths, which is much more useful. We look for 'congruency' to explore if there is a predisposition to child abuse or violence; what the guy's relational abilities are; what his impulse control is likely to be under stress. We are also looking for reliability and groundedness.

'Congruency' is established by interviewing the volunteer, his partner, a female relative, his boss, a friend and his doctor, along with doing a police check. We look at him in group settings and in his own home. We look and we listen very carefully. What we're looking for is for everyone to pretty much say the same things about the guy; for example, if his partner says he's slow to anger we'd be wanting to hear that from his boss as well. We want to know he's who he says he is. Because what we know is that sexual abusers have a 'hole' in their psyche that is traceable. If we find a hole, we will not accept him. End of story. He doesn't have to be an angel but he does have to be safe.

We realise that parents cannot go through this rigorous screening with every new person their son comes in contact with—nor should they have to. There are lots of really great, safe people out there that your boy will benefit hugely from coming into contact with, and you can't let your fears control his growing interest in the world. So it comes down to what you can do to help make him safe.

Firstly, make sure your relationship is strong enough for him to tell you if he feels uncomfortable around someone, and don't shame or bully him out of those feelings. Don't teach him to override his fears about someone because the more he learns to trust his instincts, the safer he'll be and the better he'll do in life. You could also support him by staying with him when he is around the person he feels uncomfortable about, if he has to see them for some reason (maybe it is a relative or coach). See what you pick up. Ask around. In the end, if a man doesn't feel right for you or your son, just say 'no' politely to the relationship. You may have got it wrong but who cares—it's about reducing risk.

Some clues for spotting possible child groomers:

- He will be a little too enthusiastic to earn your trust; be a little too helpful, kind, etc.
- You may feel he is running the relationship; talking over you a little or just talking too much.
- He may give you or your boy gifts a little too early on and too often.

- He may try to arrange moments alone with your boy a little too often, or out of context. He drives your boy to sport and back—fair enough—but he then wants to add in other excursions after sport, or invents other reasons to be alone with your boy that are out of context.
- Compared to other men you know, he over-communicates— too many messages, texts, calls, etc.

Women are great networkers, so you can carefully check out people you or your son feel uncomfortable about—do your own screening! Remember the six degrees of separation rule—someone always knows someone who knows someone, and if you scratch hard enough you'll find out something.

You could also have a rule that your son doesn't go to any stranger's house without permission—you have to have at least met them before he can play/stay there.

It's not about cotton-wooling your son—there are risks and then there are *risks*! Sure you want to encourage him to take managed physical and mental risks as he grows up, but you don't want to unwittingly encourage him to take sexual risks—that's a given.

A rule we made with our kids was if they were staying at a friend's place and felt unsafe at any point, they just had to tell the friend's parent—often the mother—they didn't feel well and wanted to go home. We agreed we'd go and pick them up if they did this—no debate, regardless of what we had going on. It only happened once but we think it encouraged the kids to trust their instincts and act on them—and that's a really good life lesson. Too often we feel uncomfortable about a situation and shove the feeling down in order not to appear impolite or a sookie. Stuff that—safety first.

Peer pressure

It's called peer 'pressure' because it involves everything from subtle persuasion to strong-arm tactics. Unfortunately, boys are generally more susceptible to it than girls. You may get to watch in wonder as your boy goes from being a kid who cared not a jot about what he wore to a mirror-hogging narcissist you barely recognise—obsessed about his clothes, his fringe, his emergent pimples, his teeth, the way he walks, looks and talks. Don't be fooled by the seemingly ambivalent persona—he's watching his peer group closely to figure out how he's going to begin the walk into his teenage years.

So, when does it start? Basically, peer pressure begins as soon as kids start to pay attention to what other kids think about them. That can be anywhere from about the age of five onwards. It's probably not peaking in this 8- to 11-year-old age group but it may gear up from now on. The truth is it will likely influence your boy—to greater or lesser degrees—throughout his life, just as it does all of us. Honestly, who of us isn't influenced by our peers? Whether it's buying new clothes, cars and houses, or honing our political opinions—we are influenced to some degree by the people we socialise and work with. True individualistic free spirits are a very rare breed!

American psychologist Brett Laursen says in an audio podcast on the Speaking of Psychology website that boys are more susceptible to peer pressure because they spend much more time in groups than girls, who tend to spend their time in friendship 'dyads', or pairs. 'And so,' says Dr Laursen, 'the influence that boys receive is much more likely to be concerned with fitting into the group as a whole.'

These peer-pressure forces can centre around anything from what he wears to what sport he plays and what he watches/plays online.

Later, peer pressure will influence his alcohol and drug use, his sex life and his driving habits. That's when the stakes become much higher.

Fortunately, there's a lot of groundwork you can put in as parents that will hopefully enable him to make better decisions about these more critical issues, and we'll explore that more later (see 'Staying connected' on page 151). Needless to say, it's all about—you guessed it—communication!

From the ages of about 8 to 11, your boy's friendships are often with same-gender peers and are usually based on proximity and common interests or hobbies, says American psychologist Dr Kay Trotter in an article on the Kaleidoscope Counseling website. 'Girls usually have fewer, but emotionally closer, friends than boys. Formation of exclusive "clubs" and shifting peer alliances are common at this age and media influences and popular culture increasingly affect the child's peer activities and relationships.'

Kids who don't have a lot of friends are more susceptible to peer pressure, says Dr Trotter, because they will want to protect the friendships they have. They're more likely to do what the friends they do have tell them to.

But it's also true that some people are more influential than others. If your child hangs around with people who tend to be particularly influential, they will look susceptible even though they might not be. Gotta watch those influencers—for the good and the bad.

The main thing is to keep talking to your boy about the influences he is encountering everywhere. Of course, some of the most powerful influences come from the intensive marketing efforts of people wanting to sell you stuff. We nearly drove our kids crazy by analysing television adverts: 'They're just ads!' they'd wail, as we pointed out the subliminal messages in Coca-Cola ads about becoming beautiful people with amazing lives that included dancing on exotic beaches with their hundreds of best friends. How annoying was that?! But the point is to help kids identify influences and encourage them to think about whether they want to be, do, drink, eat, wear, etc. whatever the clever marketing people are suggesting to them. Our job as parents is to help them identify and form their own values, ethics and desires, and support them to stay strong in them—even when the pressure heats up.

Talk about how peer pressure was for you and what you gave away to belong to a certain group or person. How did it feel when all your mates went into the dairy and stole lollies but you didn't? Did they exclude you from the group? How did that feel? Maybe research some strategies together around what he can say if he wants to buck a trend, and make sure you follow up on how he went. Just keep talking.

And remember, not all peer pressure is bad peer pressure. Keep an eye out for the good influencers in your boy's life and really endorse and support them. Some organisations use peer educators to teach younger kids about safe drug and alcohol use and safe sex because the reality is they'll take a whole lot more notice of their peers than they will of you. Make influencers your friends!

Let's talk about sex

It's best not to leave talking about sex with your boy too long because the reality is he's acutely aware of it—he's been getting erections since he was a baby and has become increasingly interested in them. *Very* interested!

Marry that with the fact that boys are now maturing sexually up to two years earlier than they did a few decades ago and you know it's time to talk. On average, researchers found that boys experience the beginnings of genital growth, testicular enlargement and those first stray pubic hairs between nine and ten years old nowadays. Why? One theory is rising levels of childhood obesity, as the hormones that regulate sexual development are stored in fat.

The basic rundown on puberty is this: sometime between the ages of 9 and 15, the brain starts to release the gonadotropin-releasing hormone, or GnRH for short, that kicks off puberty. When GnRH reaches the pituitary gland (a pea-shaped gland that sits just under the brain), it releases into the bloodstream two more puberty hormones—luteinising hormone (LH) and follicle-stimulating hormone (FSH). Boys and girls have both of these hormones—they just work on different parts of the body during puberty.

In boys, these hormones signal the testes to begin producing both the hormone testosterone and sperm. Testosterone is what causes most of the changes in a boy's body during puberty, and of course he'll need sperm to reproduce.

Boys begin to have wet dreams when they reach puberty. Their first ejaculation may happen during a wet dream and he may have no idea what's happened when he wakes up! So it's important to talk to him about the possibility of this before it happens. Tell him it's a normal part of growing up—that he can't control it and it's nothing to be ashamed of. It's all part of becoming a man.

Despite all these major hormonal changes signalling sexual maturation, parents seem reluctant to step up to the plate when it comes to talking to their kids about sex. A recent UK survey of 2000 parents showed that over a third of parents had *never* discussed it with their kids. Don't be one of those parents! Of the others who had, 27 per cent first discussed sex before their children were 10.

Because girls have periods, mothers—mainly—can't really avoid talking about puberty, but talking to sons can be harder, for both mothers and fathers. The main thing is to check out your son's readiness for information—let him be the driver of it.

A word of warning, though: I (Ruth) remember as a nine-year-old being sat down by my mother, who was separating from my father and about to leave the family home, to be told about the 'birds and the bees'. Call me naïve, but she might as well have been talking Congolese because I didn't have a clue what she was on about! So, you do need to consider 'ripeness' here—is he ready for the information—and the discussion needs to be led by your son. How worldly and inquisitive is he? Is he interested in sex? What does he already know, and how much and what type of information does he need from you?

Your son may also be noticing other boys' erections as well as enjoying his own, and joining in the 'boner, stiffy, woody, wang' jokes at school from around the age of six—if he's an early bird. So it's best to start explaining erections to your boy in a low-key way, making sure he understands there's nothing shameful about a natural bodily response he has not one jot of control over.

Our advice is to use the correct terms for body parts from the get-go; naming them during bathtime is a good way to do this. Moving your boy away from the euphemistic terms he's picked up will make it easier when it comes to having more serious discussions on puberty and sex.

Remember, you're not looking for the right moment to have the 'big sex talk'—in fact, all the advice points to looking for 'teachable moments', everyday situations that provide opportunities to teach your boy about topics related to sex. For example, if there's a pregnancy or new baby in the family, seize the opportunity to talk about how babies are conceived and born. The 'where do babies come from?' questions can start from as early as three or four and they need plain, clear answers. 'Mums have a uterus inside their tummies, where babies live until they are big enough to be born', etc., will do for a start but of course, you'll need more sophisticated answers as he develops.

By this age your boy's knowledge will be a mix of what he's learned at home, in the classroom and in the playground. You can start by finding out what he already knows by checking out what he's learning at school. Sex education is part of the Health and Physical Education curriculum in New Zealand. It starts in primary school covering things like friendships, different kinds of families and respect for each other and people who are different from them. In the latter years of primary they will likely cover puberty, body development and image, human reproduction and social-media risks and issues. By secondary school they are learning about positive and supportive intimate relationships, contraception, managing their health and the influence that society has on the way we view things like gender and sexuality. Find out when and how the school discusses reproduction, sexually transmitted diseases, sexual orientation, sexual harassment, and so on. If they use textbooks or handouts, read them yourself.

Then check out what he's looking at online, seeing in comics and magazines and on TV, and listening to on radio—basically just hang out with him and absorb a bit of his world so you get a handle on what and who he's referencing from. You may be very surprised! Parents we know discovered their 13-year-old was accessing violent pornography that they'd never even imagined existed. Exposure to it skewed his sexual maturation and required a lot of input from both the parents and a counsellor to unbundle the exposure.

The reality is he's probably going to check out pornography, like most of us have at some point. The danger for boys is that it will shape their perceptions of sex and relationships. Seeing images of adults having sex with children and/or animals is just plain damaging, and even some of the so-called 'soft porn' has a very unreal quality to it. Shaved genitals, bleached arseholes, whopper penises and breasts the size of balloons are simply not the stuff of everyday sexual relationships—it's unreal and sends all the wrong messages about intimacy and pleasure. Ultimately, pornography isn't about relationships—it's about power, which might be OK to explore within an adult relationship where there's no power imbalance, but it's just plain bad for young boys. The problem is pornography is everywhere and boys can easily access it online.

If you discover your boy is accessing pornography, be careful not to guilt him out or shame him—it's important to differentiate between him being interested in sex and exploring porn as part of that drive. You don't want him to 'go underground' through guilt and shame when your goal is to open up discussion about healthy sexual relationships and encourage him in that direction.

It's a delicate walk, no doubt about it, but you need to trust that all the foundation-building you've done—particularly around his healthy mother attachment—will see him through this phase. If he respects his mother, he'll have a healthy regard for women in general and that should see him right. Trust that you can have deeper conversations with your boy about pornography and its relationship to real sex. You can do this!

Dads/men are probably going to be better at talking to boys about erections, puberty and sex than mothers/women because they've experienced them. That's just a fact. But if Dad's not there and there isn't a man who you mums trust to have this conversation with your boy, wade in. Talk to a good man you know for some advice and hit your Google button—there's lots of good info available for you both to access together and discuss whatever questions/issues he has.

Remember, the main goal of any sex talk is to communicate that sex is a very normal and natural thing. And don't overreact if your boy asks you something awkward—it may put him off coming to you again.

As boys near puberty it is common for them to start feeling awkward and/or confused about their bodies—how they stack up against their friends' bodies—and the early rumblings of attraction that can be both confusing and traumatic. Sexual orientation is much more fluid these days as people explore heterosexuality, homosexuality, bisexuality, transgenderism, gender fluidity (not identifying particularly with any gender), etc.—so get ready for the roller-coaster of your boy going on the journey to discover his sexual orientation.

Ultimately, you want him to be happy. Our experience from having interviewed over 650 men in depth about their emergent sexuality is that the more authentic men are in terms of their sexual orientation, the happier and more fulfilled lives they will lead. As parents, we're there to help our sons find their right place in the world, and their sexual orientation is a big piece of that puzzle. (See 'He's doing it' on page 170 and 'Finding his sexual compass' on page 172 for more info on when your boy becomes sexually active.)

Summary

We've established there are some big hormonal changes coming up as your boy lunges towards puberty, and he's probably beginning to feel the effects of them. So are you, no doubt! Also:

- He's interested in everything and wants to know how things work.
- He's got thousands of questions—some of them really awkward!
- He's growing about 5 to 7.5 centimetres and gaining 2 to 3 kilograms a year, including fast-growing bones—possibly giving him some grief.
- His fine motor skills are rapidly increasing.
- He needs you—particularly dads—to spend more time with him doing stuff.
- He's pushing back more—you need to start negotiating boundaries more with him.
- He's starting the walk across the 'Bridge of Adolescence'.
- Mums need to step back some.
- Find your full stop—say it once, mean it and avoid repeating it.
- Don't shame him.
- Being honest and authentic with boys establishes trust.
- Keep noticing what's emerging in your boy and encourage that.
- Spending regular and real time with your boy will pay off.
- Quality time is as much about 'being' as about 'doing'.
- Keep communicating.
- Your boy can't have too many good men in his life.
- There are ways of helping him to keep safe.
- Peer pressure is kicking in big time.
- His hormones are gearing up.
- It's time to talk about sex.
- You don't need to have the 'big sex talk'—look for 'teachable moments'.

This is a great time to really enjoy your boy and lay down strong foundations for good communication before he hits the teenage years. Everything you put in now in terms of communication and trust will pay dividends later. Remember, he's confused and possibly terrified by all these changes and he needs you right there—at his side—as he navigates this phase. He ain't gonna tell you how much he needs you alongside him—that's for sure—but believe us, he needs you more now than ever. You are his anchor in this hormonal storm—his friend, his mate, his buddy. That's a privilege—enjoy!

Excellent activities for older boys

Here's a great list of activities for older boys. Ideally your boy should experience doing them with his mum and his dad, together or separately. He will learn valuable life lessons about the different approaches men and women have to exploring, doing and achieving. If some of these things are beyond your or your partner's abilities, why not recruit a friend to help— that teaches your son that asking for help is cool.

Don't get too ambitious but at least give these activities a go—even if you and your son fail, it's still an opportunity to learn and teach. Step back a bit and reflect, with your son, on what went wrong and what you could do differently next time. Or you may just come to the conclusion you are both not quite ready to build a turbo-charged go-kart right now. All good—next year!

Remember, boys love to tinker; just mucking around trying different approaches, revising each time it doesn't work until he achieves something he thinks is cool. It may not have been what you had in mind initially but his imagination will have received a real work-out as he learns to put thinking to work for himself.

The aim is to enable your son to explore, to do, to achieve and to figure out what went right or wrong. Let him do as much as possible himself, with guidance from you as needed. It doesn't need to be perfect; let him learn from his mistakes. If you do it all yourself, sure, he will see you are master of the universe—great for your ego—but he needs to learn that he too can become a master by doing and learning.

- Teach him how to make a fire and cook over it.
- Deconstruct appliances and make new things (if you can) or just see how things work.
- Do woodwork projects together, e.g. build a birdhouse, vege-garden planter box, tree hut or go-kart, teaching the use and care of tools. Start with small projects and build up.
- Take an evening education course, e.g. first aid or CPR.
- Let him steer the car in a safe environment like an empty carpark or on private land.
- Go into the city and ride up and down the elevators in high-rise buildings, stopping off at floors where you can.
- Climb up mountains and find landmarks.
- Start a collection, e.g. stamps, rocks, etc.
- Learn how to use a telephone, how to set up a voicemail message, caller ID, etc.
- Go fishing; learn about tides, fish and use and care of fishing equipment.

- Learn to use a calculator, camera, microscope or telescope.
- Assist with homework if asked, or offer to help.
- Pursue cultural events, e.g. attend a play or live concert.
- Keep a one-week diary, discussing and comparing notes on your lives.
- Teach him about community resources, where the services are and how to access them.
- Go bicycling together; teach him about bicycle repair, maintenance and road safety.
- Open the hood of a car and point out the various parts of the engine.
- Begin auto mechanics; teach him about spark plugs, points, oil changes and how to use jumper cables.
- Take a field trip to a university or to a historic place, etc.
- Paint a piece of furniture, shed, etc.
- Go grocery shopping together—send him on missions to find things for you.
- Go to a flea market, garage sale or auction.
- Explore the internet at home, a library or cyber café.
- Learn to use an old camera—one on which nothing is automatic.
- Use a globe or Google Maps to locate friends, family, travel destinations and the locations of current events.
- Use a map or Google Maps to navigate somewhere.
- Make mini-pizzas or bread together.
- Go snowboarding.
- Make foods from around the world and learn how people live in that country.

- Build a house out of iceblock sticks and glue.
- Share some of your favourite music with each other, explaining why you like it and how it makes you want to dance or sing along.
- Have a Monopoly tournament.
- Get a chemistry set and perform your own experiments.
- Make a miniature cardboard city using old cereal boxes and other cardboard templates (you can find these on the internet).
- Learn to play a musical instrument. Keep it playful—music shouldn't be a chore!

FOUR

The wild ride: 12 to 17 years

There are three things a man must ask himself: Who am I? Where am I going? Who is going with me? The trick is to get the questions in the right order.

Sam Keen

Before we start in on all the challenging aspects of the 'wild ride', let's begin by saying teenage boys are kind of fascinating—in a grungy, grunty, spotty sort of a way. They can be funny (the old understated nod of the head), insightful (young men of few wise words), creative (especially when they want to get out of doing something) and loyal (particularly to their mates!). These are good qualities overall. Let's try to keep them at the forefront of our adult minds as we navigate this minefield because you are going to need to hang onto something positive!

A lot of parents dread these teenage years—and rightly so. It's likely to be a wild ride as testosterone (the principal male sex hormone) takes charge of your son's body, including his developing brain.

Generally, puberty begins for boys from about 11 to 12 years of age and is usually physically done by 16 to 17, but be aware that your particular boy's development will be affected by both heredity and environmental factors, including diet and exercise. And that his brain development will lag way behind his physical maturation—something you'll find hard to miss!

Somewhere between the ages of 9 and 15, he'll have a 20-fold increase in his testosterone levels, according to American neuropsychiatrist and author Dr Louann Brizendine in *The Male Brain*. 'If testosterone were beer, a nine-year-old boy would get the equivalent of about one cup a day. But by age 15, it would be equal to two *gallons* [approx. 7.6 litres] a day.' That's a lot of hormones!

This testosterone tsunami will 'biologically masculinise all the thoughts and behaviours that emerge from his brain', writes Dr Brizendine. 'It will stimulate the rapid growth of male brain circuits that were formed before he was born. It will also enlarge his testicles, activate the growth of his muscles and bones, make his beard and pubic hair grow, deepen his voice, and lengthen and thicken his penis.'

Around the age of 11 or 12—when he is in Year 7 and 8 in New Zealand—your boy's sleep clock will also be affected by these hormones. He may piss you off when he starts staying up late and sleeping all morning, but the truth is he can't help it. 'Testosterone receptors reset his brain's clock cells,' writes Dr Brizendine. 'By the time a boy is fourteen, his new sleep set point is pushed an hour later than that of girls his age.' Her research shows this is just the beginning of boys being out of sync with girls—from now on he'll go to sleep and wake up later than his female peers until they go through menopause.

This altered sleep pattern means most teenage boys end up surviving on only 5 to 6 hours' sleep a night when their brains require at least 10 to function optimally. The experts recommend parents unplug the internet at night if they want their boys to get to sleep and advise schools to shunt out start times a couple of hours if they really want teenage boys to learn. Seems sensible to us. (See 'Secondary school and university—making good decisions' on page 159.)

While the human body has gone through most of its physical changes by about the age of 17, new research shows the brain doesn't finish developing until about 25—some say as late as 28 for males. That's why insurance companies set 25 as the benchmark for when adult insurance rates kick in, because that's when we start being capable of making better decisions. It also why many think the driving age should be raised to 18 or even 21.

Dr Frances Jensen is an American neurologist and neuroscientist—and also a solo parent with two sons. She turned her research lens onto the development of the teenage brain after her sons hit adolescence and their behaviour became erratic—clever in some areas and really crazy in others. Dr Jensen told Radio New Zealand National she decided to look for some facts in an effort to explain their behaviour, and her research uncovered a treasure trove of information.

Over the last 10 or so years she has discovered that the brain is, indeed, the last organ in your body to develop fully. 'Teenagers are not adults with fewer miles on them—they may look big and strong or fully mature on the outside but their brains are only about 80 per cent of the way there,' said Jansen. Cause and effect are simply not hard-wired yet.

The author of *The Teenage Brain: A Neuroscientist's Survival Guide to Raising Adolescents and Young Adults*, Dr Jensen said the frontal lobes of the brain which drive rational thinking are not fully connected in teenagers, so they access information more slowly than adults. They don't have as much myelin—a fatty coating that enables nerve signals to flow freely between different parts of the brain (also known as 'white matter'; think insulation on an electrical wire)—as adults and this lack of myelin leads to inefficient communication between different parts of the brain. Jensen said in teenagers, the frontal lobe—the seat of executive function that governs judgement, insight, impulse control and empathy—is the last to be fully connected to the rest of the system, not until the mid-twenties. 'Judgement is simply not built into their brains yet which makes them very adventurous!'

According to Dr Brizendine in *The Male Brain*, the hormones testosterone and vasopressin (which new evidence suggests plays an important role in social behaviour and sexual motivation) actually alter a teenage boy's sense of reality. 'A key purpose of a hormone is to prime new behaviours by modifying our brain's perceptions,' she writes. '[B]oys hormones prime them for aggressive and territorial behaviours. As he reaches manhood, these behaviours will aid him in defending and aggressively protecting his loved ones. But first, he will need to learn how to control these innate impulses.'

These massive hormonal changes will drastically affect his frontal lobe function—specifically his higher mental processes such as thinking, decision-making and planning. Oh dear! The frontal lobe also regulates memory, impulse control and planning for the future, and stops us doing things that may cause harm.

What's happening during the teenage years is the brain is constructing itself—laying down neural pathways through experience and learning. Your beautiful boy is slowly moving away from dependence on you towards learning to manage his own life. In short, he's ramping up his skills to survive in a man's world. To do this he needs to seek out new experiences, be willing to take risks and do things that may look a whole lot like impulsive, dangerous behaviour to your mature brain. Even more frightening is all this behaviour will be strongly influenced by his social group. Be very afraid!

American neuroeconomist and author Paul J. Zak says in *The Moral Molecule* that although testosterone is present in women too, men have 10 times as much, hence their propensity for 'bad behaviour'. The 'real driver of the Bad Boy bus is the oxytocin (the happy hormone) antagonist known as testosterone,' writes Zak.

Testosterone increases muscle mass and bone density—consequently enhancing athletic performance—and also comes in useful during combat situations and anything else that requires risk-taking, physical courage, strength and speed. But the truth is, writes Zak, it also causes a hell of a lot of trouble. 'Most crimes are committed by young men, and most murderers are males in the age range of twenty to twenty-five . . . Young men have levels of testosterone that are twice the levels of older men, so the term *testosterone poisoning* for this age group is no joke.'

The big problem we face now, according to Dr Jensen, is that our environment offers a variety of tempting stimuli unprecedented in all of human culture. Teenagers have so much access to things that are risky—the internet, social networks and adventure sports we never dreamed of. '[They are] the same old teenagers but with many more tools that can lead them down very risky paths.' (See 'Social media and gaming' on page 184.)

Respite, respite, we hear you beg! OK—here's some good news. Zak also posits the theory that the happy hormone oxytocin ultimately holds the human trump card over its more competitive and aggressive sibling, testosterone. Basically, he says, oxytocin controls our moral behaviour and sustains the social cooperation that ensures survival of our species.

His experiments have proved that oxytocin is triggered naturally 'when one person extends himself to another in a trusting way'. Bingo—the person being trusted experiences a surge in oxytocin. And oxytocin generally produces generous and caring moral behaviour, which in turn produces the more moral, caring society we all want. Take that, testosterone!

We think this bodes well for our relationships with our testosterone-fuelled teenage boys. If we can keep extending the hand of trusting friendship to them, whilst simultaneously setting boundaries that help make them safe, the majority of our boys will continue to grow into fine young men—with a little help from oxytocin.

The danger zone

As they navigate these years, the danger zones are peer pressure and risk-taking around alcohol, drugs, cars, adventure sports and sex. Let's face it, alcohol and/or drugs and an underdeveloped frontal lobe is a wicked combo—and occasionally deadly. The reality is we all just hope our sons make it through and feel huge sadness for the families of the ones that don't.

There is no shortage of stories about fun turning bad. Once, as a group of teenagers, we (Ruth and friends) all went swimming in a river in the Manawatu. It was a beautiful day; the sun was shining and the river was glistening. It looked even rosier to us because we were all stoned.

Some of the guys were jumping off a high rock sticking up out of the river. No one checked the depth around it. As one of our friends floated face-down in front of us—long hair flowing around him—we all yahooed and cheered him on; amazed at how long he could hold his breath. Until we realised something was wrong . . . When we finally acted and dragged him onto the river-bank he gurgled, 'I've broken my fucking back.' And he had. We called an ambulance and that friend spent the rest of his life in a wheelchair. At least he lived.

Some don't. We had first-hand experience of a car accident in which a young man died. We will never forget the utter desolation on the faces of that boy's parents as they farewelled their beloved son.

The harsh reality is that teenagers, alcohol and cars are a lethal combination and can have a devastating effect on all involved. Enough said.

Along with increased risk-taking—as if that wasn't enough—your son is also going to experience heightened emotions during these teenage years that will make everything seem bigger than Africa to him. He'll experience incredible highs and crashing lows as he encounters new territory—individually and with his mates—often taking himself to the outer edge of his comfort zone and certainly way past yours! The greater the risk, the greater the reward. If he pulls off whatever antic he's caught up in, he's a hero—lauded by his mates. But risk and shame share the same bed and he'll fall hard if he feels he's failed or embarrassed himself.

The intense emotions from these teenage years stay with us for the rest of our lives. The songs we'll all sing in our rest homes will be from these heady days because we feel emotions so deeply at that age. Our feelings are so open and raw during that time—so many positive emotions; so much despair and heartache. It brings to mind a quote from American rock legend John Hiatt, recalling when he first heard fellow singer-songwriter Bob Dylan's classic 1965 anthem 'Like a Rolling Stone': 'I still remember where I was when I first heard it. I heard it on the car radio while waiting for my mom to come out of a drugstore in Monticello, Indiana. I remember feeling that when she got back in the car, she wouldn't recognise me.'

This illustrates well the huge internal development going on in your son around forming his identity (who am I?) at this age, and it's happening at a galloping pace. In fact, you may actually not recognise your son at times; you may think, 'He's not the sweet boy he used to be,' but this is good (no, really, it is!). It's a good measure that he is busy at work forming up his identity, his authentic self. For this identity to be healthy, it will not necessarily be an extension of his parents or even remotely what you would like.

It's about now you may need to remember that archetype you saw in him when he was young, that uniqueness you tried to support. You may recognise that uniqueness fully coming into being, so we say, stay faithful to the glimpse you caught of your son when he was young; try to stand alongside him as he valiantly struggles to form an authentic self.

As a rightly concerned parent you may find it very easy to become the enemy in that battle. Occasionally, being the enemy may provide your son with a solid reference point to bounce off, but try not to make it a habit. We think that as a parent, it's really important at this age and stage to try to hold the longer-term perspective and give him some slack at times, and at other times to hold the line strong.

But above all, try to be alongside him, rather than blocking from the front or pushing from behind.

The power of adolescence

Adolescence certainly has a power. At this time adults—parents in particular—seem like dinosaurs from another planet with nothing to offer but their outdated, narrow views on just about everything.

I (Ruth) can remember being at my grandparents' house watching the 1969 Woodstock festival unfold on television. I was a 14-year-old rebel-in-waiting—absolutely fascinated by these long-haired, flower-wearing, peace-loving anarchists thumbing their noses at the establishment I'd already decided held nothing of interest to me. My grandfather threw himself in front of the television, yelling, 'You love them, don't you? You love those hippies!' I just looked at him and thought, 'Yep. Those are my people.' There was no turning back!

Many of us have these seminal, often euphoric moments during our teenage years that send us off on previously unimagined paths and go a long way to forming the adults we will become. Some people say it's a throw of the dice what comes our way and others say we make our own luck. Whatever, ultimately, it all comes down to how we process what happens to us; how we make sense of events and what we do with the knowledge gleaned from them. That's where parents come in!

The flip side of all these heightened emotions is, of course, when the emotions are negative or frightening, they are felt equally deeply. Your boy may not say or show too much, but a rebuff from a friend—particularly a girl or boy he fancies—will plunge him into a silent despair that can be alarming. Stay close to this. He can't tell you he needs you but you're his safety rail right now—he needs to know you are close alongside him for him to feel safe.

So how do we help our teenage boys understand their vulnerabilities? Dr Jensen decided to give her sons facts because they are an information, facts-based group: she says teenagers are learning machines who love data and information. Adults, who do have developed frontal lobes, can help them think through causality. 'Remember, they are receptive to good and bad stimuli and information,' Dr Jensen told Radio New Zealand National.

This is our advice for parents of teenage boys (with a nod to Dr Jensen, Celia Lashlie et al.):

- Teach them they are late bloomers—talk hormones with them.
- Tell them nothing is fixed in stone. Don't crucify them for any errors of judgement made at 13 or 14—they aren't an indicator of future behaviour because your boy is still developing.
- Don't take a laissez-faire approach to parenting, e.g. 'I'll just muddle along until he's 21 or 22 and it will all be all right.' Stay active in his life. Keep alongside him.
- Set boundaries without ripping the fun out of his world. He's heavily committed to fun.
- Try not to alienate your son—don't just get angry with him and lock him out. You have to stay connected to him to know if he's playing with fire.
- Start to take a real interest in who his friends are and build some relationship with them. Make your place the go-to destination without it becoming the party house (other parents won't thank you for providing party central).

- Know when your boy needs time alone. Give him time to dwell on things. Know when to stop talking and respect his silence.
- Keep him busy—being involved in a sport or other physical activity will help him expend testosterone and socialise. Boys are competitive and like to physically challenge each other.
- Find creative ways to spend face-to-face time with your boy. Hang out with him. Don't be put off by him pushing you away—suck it up and be creative about finding a new way to get alongside him.
- Don't project adult skill sets or self-discipline on him—you're making the boundaries until he is capable of doing it.
- Don't be a helicopter parent—he has to learn by trial and error. Think managed risks with quiet, non-emotional debriefings with him after the inevitable failures.
- If you see him playing with fire—step in. He won't like it, so be careful not to shame him, but stand strong.
- Get help if you need it—counselling is really important if your boy is becoming increasingly depressed, aggressive or isolated.
- Know that teenage boys are capable of making substantial shifts in attitude and behaviour when they need to. They are way more fluid than us oldies.

Finally, Dr Dan Siegel, clinical professor of psychiatry at the UCLA School of Medicine, says in his video 'Flipping Your Lid: A Scientific Explanation', on the Dalai Lama Center for Peace and Education's YouTube channel, that there are four key changes taking place during the teenage years: novelty seeking, social engagement, increased emotional intensity and creative explorations. 'These changes affect how teens seek rewards in trying new things, connect with their peers in different ways, feel more intense emotions and push back on the existing way of doing things to create new ways of being in the world,' Dr Siegel says.

The really interesting thing is that while studies show teenagers can describe risks as accurately as adults, they are way more likely to take them. Why? Sue Wright, executive director of the Brainwave Trust, says in an article on the trust's website that there are two reasons: 'The first is that often the gain from feeling the fear and just "doing it" outweighs the perceived risk of harm. The second is the social peer-group influences adolescents to take more risks as the feeling of reward and exhilaration is so much greater.

'Adolescence is a unique and special time, full of both risk and opportunity. The experiences they have shape their learning and their brain. It is also a time when parents are sometimes needed to perform some of the functions of the front part of the brain!'

As if we didn't have enough going on right now—we have to be their brains, as well as feed and clothe them! So hold the longer view, friends, and maybe allow yourself to feel some excitement for the heroic journey your son is taking. It's a wild ride but a critically important one in shaping your son into a healthy man. You are riding alongside your son and while the occasional speed wobble may alarm you, stay open to the sheer exhilaration of the ride—you may get something from it. That's why they call parenting character-building!

Staying connected

How do you stay in a relationship with a teenage boy who just grunts? Have faith—the consensus is he does hear what you say and appreciates what you do; he just struggles to show it. The truth is he still very much needs you to care, so don't get pissed off if he doesn't respond—it's all about staying connected, having faith and looking for the small clues that tell you he's still a nice human being.

It will involve huge effort with minimal returns. You'll be stretched to the outer limits of your humanity with monosyllabic replies to your seemingly benign, futile attempts at communication, such as: 'OK', 'Na', 'Yep', 'Dunno' and 'Whatever'. You'll analyse the shit out of those five responses before this stage is done! The desire to prise more info from your uncooperative son will likely be met with hostility— maybe even disgust—and you'll learn to suck that up as well and try again another day.

Hope and patience will become your new best friends—patience in particular, as you wait for those times where for one brief moment his door opens and he expresses what's happening inside him. It may be a quiet evening on the beach, a sudden articulate response to news, a movie or a comment, or late at night. Savour it, my friends.

One of the biggest things teenagers struggle with is how little control they have over what happens to them. They know they are living on the edge and it's frightening when they realise that bad things can happen to good people—including them. What we ultimately want to teach our young men is that what they *do* have is almost total control over how they *react* to the bad things that happen to them.

That's where us parents can help. Encouraging them to speak up; being a listening ear; talking through the situation; exploring the options with them. As parents, our responsibility is to make sure they can come to us when times are bad.

Sadly, lots of teenagers say the *last* people they want to talk to are their parents—they are afraid of disappointing us or letting us down, of us freaking out. We are often the last people to hear about our son's very sad story. We need them to be able to come to us and say, 'Mum, don't freak out but . . .' Maybe if we can do a better job of listening, our boys will speak up more and we could do a lot of good things for our teenagers. Practically, that means literally not freaking out when your son comes to you with a difficult story. It means having the discipline to stay calm and listen carefully before offering pragmatic advice, a sounding board or simply a shoulder to cry on.

Another really important thing is knowing when your boy needs time alone; understanding that he processes things differently—in a non-verbal way. Remember psychologist Nigel Latta's great advice: 'Be brief. Say what you need to say then shut up.' Give him time to think about what you've said and process it in his mysteriously quiet, boy way.

The tricky balancing act here is knowing how long to give him to dwell on things and knowing when to circle back in—think of it like a gyroscope! You'll need to weigh up your need to express your thoughts/feelings about an issue and how much is too much for your boy to hear and be able to process. Trial and error, my friends! As a general rule, we think two weeks is the maximum time you can leave an issue before circling back in. For smaller issues—or bigger ones, if they are really serious—it could be as little as 24 hours.

Acclaimed young adult author Laurie Halse Anderson, whose debut novel *Speak* explored social ostracism in high schools, said in a Radio New Zealand National interview that teenagers often show fractures that are present in their family systems. 'It's bad timing because often kids are going through adolescence just as parents are beginning to go through their own mid-life crisis, which deals with many of the same issues—identity issues, changes in their bodies, examining relationships. It's very hard for parents if they are going through their own financial or emotional issues. They can't be the parent they might want to be—at a time when their kids need them the most.'

This could be confronting but Anderson, who has raised four children, said after 20 years of writing for teenagers she's gained an understanding of what makes adults tick. She said many adults have significant unresolved issues, like sexual assault or rape from adolescence, that come back to haunt them. 'I liken it to an infection; if a bad thing has happened to you and you haven't shared it and it's become a secret, holding in that secret in your soul is like not treating an infection—it grows.'

The reality is that unresolved issues inhibit your ability to parent because unprocessed emotions become fears, and it's very easy to project those fears onto your kids in unhealthy ways. The message you will give them is that the world they are so unbelievably keen to explore and experience is an unsafe place that they have neither the instincts nor the skills to survive. That's not the message boys need to receive to become healthy, happy, productive adults.

They need to feel confident you can create safe boundaries while they navigate these testosterone-fuelled years that provide both danger and opportunity in equal measure. They need to know you are right there with them—aware of what they are facing and able and willing to walk alongside them. They need your help but they also need your faith in them.

Importantly, Anderson attributes a lot of teenage risky behaviour to holding secrets about traumatic or frightening events in their lives. 'When you see kids who are regularly engaging in dangerous behaviours, it's generally because something has gone wrong. That introduces a whole other level of problems that can dog them for the rest of their life.'

She said if there are issues you are struggling to talk about with your teenage boy, research them well and put a good young adult fiction book under their noses: 'Teenagers *love* to read—they just don't like to read boring books. If you hand them a book that connects to their heart they are consumed by it—they're passionate!'

Why not movies and videos, you ask? Well, they can be helpful (especially those that elicit empathy) but reading requires engaging the imagination and it's your son's active imagination that will be one of his greatest allies in forming up character and identity. As Albert Einstein said, 'Imagination is more important than knowledge. Knowledge is limited. Imagination encircles the world.'

Anderson said parents know the world is scary and worry that if their kids read about things like sex or anorexia they'll go out and do or become those things but it's simply not true: 'Literature can start a conversation with parents that opens up the possibility of getting help if needed.'

Another important aspect in developing a healthy relationship with your boy is making sure you spend face-to-face time with him—regularly. Make time in your busy life to hang out with him—even when he starts to push you away. You just have to suck it up and be creative—find a new way to spend time with him, because he needs you more than ever now. If you fall into the bad habit of being ships that pass in the night—with him diving into his mobile or onto his computer and going off to his bedroom—that's a recipe for disaster if you're trying to be an effective, loving parent.

It doesn't need to be big amounts of time but it does need to be regular and often. If you are struggling for ideas to gain this time, think food—he will usually be more than willing to eat, even more so if you provide the food, which gives you a chance to connect between mouthfuls.

If you've tried everything to stay connected to your son and he's becoming increasingly depressed, aggressive or isolated—get help. Ask around for recommendations for a good counsellor and do whatever it takes to get him there. A friend of ours bribed her 13-year-old grandson with the promise of new shoes if he went to a counsellor after he became very aggressive and isolated. He clicked with the male counsellor and never looked back. He was able to identify why he was angry and that insight allowed him to change his behaviour. Got the new shoes too!

If your boy is unwilling to do face-to-face counselling, try arranging phone or even email counselling as a starting point. Oh, and you will have to arrange it—don't expect him to.

We believe the interpersonal skills gained through counselling will also serve him well in later life—when or if he comes unstuck around relationship issues, children, career crises, etc. (See 'Reaching out for help' on page 192.)

Cutting the cord

Celia Lashlie's outstanding insights into teenage boys were based on both her experiences working in New Zealand prisons and talking with thousands of boys in classrooms throughout the country as part of her Good Man Project. The international bestseller that came out of that project—*He'll Be OK: Growing Gorgeous Boys into Good Men*—was written as an exploration of 'how we could all work together more effectively to keep young men safe as they ride the roller-coaster that is male adolescence'. It was also 'to honour men, their skill, their intuition, their pragmatism and their humour and their extraordinary ability to become boys again at a moment's notice, whatever their age'.

We believe the main reason Lashlie's book was such a huge success was because her advice to mothers to 'get off the bridge' and allow boys to grow up through experiencing risk (see page 111) was radical but right. Someone needed to say it and that someone was Celia Lashlie. And, let's face it—it had to come from a woman!

The 'bridge of adolescence' she identified runs from ages 11 to 18. From 11 to 12 years it's all about boys making friends—finding their mates; 13 to 14 requires tight rule-making from parents; and from 15 to 18 the rules slowly diminish as boys step into early manhood. The opportunities to fall off the bridge involve sex, drugs, cars and alcohol.

The premise is that good men need to be clearly visible at the edge and other side of the bridge as boys make the passage into manhood. And mothers need to encourage their sons onto the bridge—knowing those good men are there—and trust they will 'be OK'. 'It's not about mothers abandoning their sons; it's about them accepting that for a time they will walk beside the bridge of adolescence rather than on it, or if they can't quite manage to stay off the bridge, that they at least commit to walking on one side rather than marching down the centre line directing traffic.' Who—us?! Sorry, mums—we know every instinct in your body wants to protect your son but you can still do it in other ways. By ensuring there are good men close to him; by him knowing you are there and ready if he needs you; by having faith in him and trust in all the great work you put in from birth.

Our experience at Big Buddy supports the idea that there is a time for mothers to step back and for fathers to step up—if they are in the boy's life. We start getting desperate calls from mums as their sons hit 14 to 15, saying they are losing control. Programme manager Steve Sobota reports mums often say their boy has lost interest in his sport—he's just not motivated to do it anymore.

'He's more in his room playing computer games and is more isolated from his friends. Mum's trying to impart her wisdom and get her boy to do things, and he's just saying "no". It's a turning point in their relationship. Mums become more desperate and worried at this stage. And unfortunately, it's usually too late for us to get involved.'

If his dad isn't around, we suggest you look for another good man you trust—who can engage with your son—hopefully before he turns 12. We find that by around the age of 12 to 13, boys seem to really question having a mentor, and the window of opportunity for them to engage with a man narrows dramatically. 'Unfortunately,' says Sobota, 'there is often some sort of shutting down by then if they haven't already established a relationship with a good man. I have an image of a young man walking away from that male light that can take him down a certain path to manhood.'

Sobota says when he meets the 12- to 14-year-old boys whose desperate mothers have begged for help, their attitude about having a mentor is, 'If this is Mum's idea, it's a bad idea.' 'They want to be more independent but they don't really know what they want either—it's a bit of a no-man's-land. These are the boys who have grown themselves into men and they are going to struggle—they are much more likely to have problems with authority figures, and go through jobs and relationships. Youth suicide is a high risk for these boys.' (See 'Suicide and mental illness' on page 187.)

Hopefully, your son already has these adult men in his life, so now is the time for them to step up. Most men know this is their time—hey, they went through the same trials when they were teenagers. Some men may just need reminding, and now is good.

Secondary school and university— making good decisions

Thinking about the work world your boy will walk into and what skills he'll need to prosper in it is a hard ask when you're busy surviving in it yourself. But think about it you must, because your understanding of the future will inform the decisions you make about his education. This is important, people, really important.

Generally speaking, decisions on secondary schooling will likely flow on from the choices you made at primary level, but now you know so much more about your son. You have a much better idea about his academic skills and needs, his socialisation and his personality. In what school environment does he function and flourish best? Single-sex or co-educational, rule-based or liberal, self-directed learning or more structured, boarding or day pupil, traditional or alternative philosophy?

One place to start is to think about what the purpose of education is: are you wanting your son's education focused on learning for the sake of learning, or for a future career—or both? Do you imagine he'll have a number of career changes throughout his working life? If so, what skills will he need to survive and prosper in these possibly divergent work environments? And what sort of working world do you think he'll inhabit? Because as we said earlier, what we do know is that it won't look anything like the one we inhabit now!

We will repeat that because it's so crucial. *The work world your son will eventually enter will not look anything like the work world you entered.*

Digest this:

- Experts believe half of today's jobs will be completely redundant by 2025.
- Artificial intelligence will mean that many jobs will be done by computers.
- Workspaces with rows of desks will no longer exist.

Welcome to the world of artificial intelligence, my friends!

A recent report by consulting firms CBRE and Genesis predicts customer services, process work and vast swathes of middle management will simply 'disappear'. We can expect everything from self-driving cars to 'carebots' for the elderly as rapid advances in technology present a threat to many jobs normally performed by people. 'A revolutionary shift in the way workplaces operate is expected to take place over the next 10 to 15 years, which could put some people's livelihoods at risk,' says the report. Let's put that into chilling context. If your son is 12 now, when he hits a really workable age— say 22—the workplace will be one you simply will not recognise.

This is supported by 'futurist' Graeme Codrington at British change-consulting firm TomorrowToday Global who said in a *Daily Mail Online* article: 'In the last two centuries, we've seen two significant shifts in the global labour market. First we stripped the agricultural sector of workers, and then we did the same to manufacturing. Now the machines are coming for the tertiary sector, and will begin to strip companies of their white-collar workers in the next decade.'

New jobs will, of course, be created, and what future generations are going to need are transferrable skills that will enable them to be agile as they navigate this moving employment landscape so unimaginable to us. But hey, if we'd asked our great-grandparents if they thought the telephone would get traction, they might have responded as an employee at Western Union did in an internal memo of 1878: 'This "telephone" has too many shortcomings to be seriously considered as a practical form of communication. The device is inherently of no value to us.' Or, if we'd asked our grandparents about the future of computers, they might have said: 'There is no reason for any individual to have a computer in their home,' as did Kenneth Olsen, president and founder of Digital Equipment Corporation in 1977. 'Nuff said!

Vice-chancellor of Auckland University of Technology (AUT) Derek McCormack said in a *New Zealand Herald* interview that collaboration will be the most desired skill as people negotiate agreements between and within networks, rather than being a 'worker ant' in a hierarchy. It's already happening, he said. 'Employers are increasingly wanting people who are strong in a number of fields, including communication, critical reasoning, cultural awareness, creativity, curiosity, collaboration, cooperation, coping with complexity and caring within a sense of community—graduates who have a good range of what I call "C-skills".'

Employers need people who are going to work well in teams, get on well with colleagues and think carefully about the quality of their work, said McCormack. 'Big international companies like Google, Facebook and Apple are ignoring exam results—they have their own tests for prospective employees centred around "C-skills". That's not to say grades don't matter—getting good grades is a great aspiration to have—but exam results are only one measure; employers are looking out for good all-rounders.'

Importantly, McCormack said the roots of acquiring good 'C-skills' go back to early play and socialisation. Obviously the better the skills acquired in childhood, the better chance of building on them later, so it is really good to encourage and nurture early sociali-sation skills in your boys (which is why we banged on about this so much in previous chapters).

In a recent article in *The Guardian,* John Newbigin, chair of Creative England, said people who are innovative and creative, and who can think laterally, communicate clearly and work as part of a team, have abilities that are most effectively developed in children through the arts and music. A study of entrepreneurial digital busi-nesses in and around Brighton by the Arts and Humanities Research Council showed that companies whose staff had a balance between those with an arts background and those with a technology background were growing at three times the rate of less balanced companies.

'But forget about jobs and the economy,' Newbigin said, 'the real evidence, and all of us know it, is that the way children get set up for life is by having balance, variety and stimulus in their lives and in their education—well-rounded, to use a very traditional phrase.'

New York University philosophy teacher Kwame Anthony Appiah, who visited New Zealand to deliver the 2013 Sir Douglas Robb lectures, said in a *New York Times* interview that there's a worldwide shift in focus in tertiary education away from the 'Utopia Univer-sity'—the older idea of a university providing liberal education of citizens, with a focus on culture and society and being a safe place of free speech. 'Modern universities are drifting towards a "Utility University" [model] where students are customers wanting to enhance their careers,' he said. 'They are more interested in the development of their skills and salaries rather than their souls, and "value" rather than "values". Most universities in New Zealand are sitting somewhere in the middle of this tension but moving rapidly towards the utility side. Learning the "C-skills" is what's really important here.'

Appiah identifies the need for cultural competencies as diasporas morph, shifting people around the world, so employees increasingly need to be able to work with different cultures—worth noting.

These 'C-skills' won't just be needed by graduates coming out into the professional sector either—tradies will need really good collaboration skills as they liaise closely with other tradies. It used to be, for example, that a house was built by one builder with an apprentice hammer-hand, with the electrician and plumber coming in when needed. But now there are specialised concreters, footing installers, cladders, roofers, window fitters, plasterers, electricians, digital specialists, security experts and landscapers—and that's not to mention all the suppliers and building regulators. So tradespeople have to be able to work with each other in complex project schedules.

The biggest questions are around whether our secondary schools and universities can or will keep pace with changing employment needs and what you, as parents, can do to make sure your boy both retains a love of knowledge and learning and is employable and self-supporting sometime before you are ready to retire!

Our best advice when it comes to choosing a secondary school and university for your son is still to talk long and hard as a family about what aspirations he has for his future, and what educational environments are most likely to help him achieve these goals. What type of kid is he? Does he love learning for the pure sake of it? Is he a natural salesman? Or was he born for the stage? Maybe he just loves making things—using his hands and his head to create stuff. You may notice he is a linchpin in his social group, indicating that he is developing the social skills that will be critical in finding a job later.

The more activities you do together, the more of a handle you'll get on what excites him. Then you'll have to figure out whether it's a passion and a vocation or something he's happy to have as a hobby while he focuses on a career. That's an important dance right there. Notice and encourage but don't get fixated on any particular interest as career potential.

There is a bit of a movement away from the academic-road-for-all song sheet of recent decades in favour of apprenticeships and trades training. The Ministry of Education funds trades academies that focus on delivering trades and technology programmes to secondary students based on partnerships between schools, tertiary institutions, industry training organisations and employers.

According to the Ministry of Education, the purpose of a trades academy is to:

- motivate more students to stay engaged in learning and training by providing them with a greater number of options for study
- provide students with clear pathways post-school by giving them a head-start on training for vocational qualifications and smooth access to employment
- improve the responsiveness of schools to business and economic needs.

If this sounds like your boy, discuss it with the secondary schools you are considering for him; it will give you a steer on their commitment to this path before you take the plunge.

If he's sporty and has ambitions in that direction, find a school that has a strong focus on sports but make sure his education is well-rounded—he won't be a top-level athlete forever, regardless of his ambitions. Make sure he participates in a mix of individual and team sports, and non-competitive sports like tramping, so he's acquiring some of those 'C-skills' and rounding out his character. Oh, and a reminder—be very sure it's *his* interest in sports we are talking about—not yours. Sorry, but it's not his job to fulfil your unmet wishes for the fame of an amazing sports career.

Similarly, if his focus is on the arts—drama, music, dance, fine arts, etc.—find a school and university that both plays to his strengths and sees value in the place of arts in a material world. You can probably hear your old granddad saying, 'There's no money in art.' Sorry, Granddad—it's all changed and you are wrong.

We advise you spend some time acquainting yourself with both the New Zealand National Curriculum and the labyrinth that is the National Certificate of Educational Achievement (NCEA), which is the national senior secondary school qualification. Your boy will usually be assessed during his last three years at school (years 11 to 13). He can achieve NCEA at three levels in a wide range of courses and subjects that will take him on to tertiary study. Just be aware that the pathways to tertiary study start early—check out your boy is on the right path before he finds out that if he didn't study 'X' at high school, he can't study 'Y' at a technical institute or university. It can be very frustrating but remember also that most tertiary institutes run foundation courses and short courses that may help your son catch up to degree entry-level if necessary.

You may also want to check out the number of male teachers in a school—some have higher ratios than others. In the past 10 years the number of male teachers in both primary and secondary schools has dropped. In 2013, men made up only 41.2 per cent of secondary/high school teachers in New Zealand—better than the 16.5 per cent of primary school teachers but not optimal. Big Buddy programme manager Steve Sobota says it's an issue. 'Ten years ago there was a lot of discussion around male teacher numbers dropping off and what should be done about it but I haven't seen any movement—if anything, it's got worse.

'There were a lot more male teachers when I was at school; I remember one of my favourite teachers was male. He had this really cool V8 car and he did things that were really off the wall—like going outside for some classes, or he'd just pick up his guitar and start singing in class. We thought he was cool! We still got through the work but it was more fun and that's really important—for boys, fun is critical.

'Making learning creative and fun and interesting is really impor-tant for boys—doing it in a more creative way than the linear textbook way. Kinaesthetic learning just seems to work better for boys. I really like the idea of boys' classes and girls' classes within a co-ed school. I don't know why we don't do it more.'

Finally, your son has potentially five years at secondary school and upwards of three years at tertiary level—if it's not working for him and you've tried everything from changing teachers to changing subjects, be prepared to change schools—that's the power you have as parents. They'll moan and kick off but they'll eventually settle—you just have to trust yourself and ride it out.

How annoying is he!

Every generation has its particularly annoying trends. We drove our parents and teachers crazy with our long hair, bare feet, wide bell-bottom jeans, Gandhi jackets and anti-establishment attitudes. Our son's punk attire—complete with safety pins and a dyed mohawk—was a mystery to us. Parents no doubt struggled with the hair-over-eyes, pants-down-round-arses and untied shoelaces era. (Oh, the temptation to tell them pull their pants up!) Then there was the ripped jeans, dirty T-shirt, couldn't-care-less grunge look. And now we've got long T-shirts, yoga pants and—who would've thought?—beards are back in for older boys! On it goes.

Just know that whatever he's going through is a phase—it'll pass. A lot of young men become very conscious of how they look at about the age of 12 or 13 and are heavily influenced by their peers. They'll try out different trends until they find one they are comfortable with—and that could be based solely on which one pisses you off the most.

The take-away here is the less you react, the more quickly it will pass. We're not saying this is easy—just grit your teeth and bear it as best you can. We once went to a punk gig by our son's band in the bowels of West Auckland—we stuck out like dogs' balls and were hearing-impaired for days afterwards but when we talked to him after the gig, he was his usual lovely self and really pleased we'd come.

The other sure-fire way to make a phase pass quickly is, of course, to start dressing the same way as your son. If he thinks you think it's cool, it'll be gone by lunchtime!

Harder to handle is the rancid-sock-smelling-bedroom phase that usually peters out by about 16 to 18 but can last up to age 30 these days—appalling as that sounds! (See *Go west, young man: 18-plus* on page 200.) There are different ways to deal with this: if it doesn't really bother you, just spray, shut the door to his room and walk away. As long as vermin don't colonise the rest of the house, it's his problem, really. However, regardless of his age, it's your house and if you don't want to live with his creeping cesspit, Nigel Latta's advice still stands (see page 114). If your 18-plus big boy doesn't like living at Colditz, he's free to move out!

We also think that if boys have a solid male influence in their lives—hopefully by the time they are seven—by the time they hit this age and stage, they've got enough 'relationship money' in the bank to weather this patch. Men are also generally more tolerant and much better at the short, sharp 'just do it' instructions that mothers sometimes tend to overwork—just a tad. Let's be honest—if he hasn't responded to the first three requests, he's unlikely to act on the next 30!

So strategise over who is going to confront the unlovely behaviours that come with adolescence. Figure out who is most likely to get the required result—even if it's not up to Mum's exacting standards. Learn to live with the C grade, mothers! As we have said before, pick your battles.

If his father isn't there to support your fair requests, talk to a man your boy respects and ask him to help. At Big Buddy we get numerous reports from mums saying they'd been asking their son to do such-and-such for ages, and then all it took was a few words from their mentor and bang—job done! Frustrating for mums, but the reality is boys are not generally looking for their mother's approval in the same way they seek affirmation from 'the man', whose approval is very much associated with a boy growing himself into manhood.

Finding the good

Despite his best, heroic efforts to conceal his finer qualities, you know and see the best in your boy. You know the kid under whatever persona he is currently trying out and it's really important to be as faithful to that archetype of his true spirit as you can be. Remember his kindness, softness, inquisitiveness, creativity, humour, loyalty, maybe his leadership qualities—whatever it is about your son that you respect and admire. Because he will mature, and with the right along-siding through these turbulent years, you'll see all his fine qualities emerge in the man he becomes and you'll burst with pride! Hey, we feel your pain—we are just reminding you there is a light at the end of this troubling dark tunnel and that light is your son, as an amazing man.

Find ways to praise both your own son and all the adolescent boys you know. It is especially important that men do this. The Jungian psychoanalyst Robert Moore put it more bluntly: 'If an older man isn't blessing a younger man then he is harming him.'

Try to notice the smallest things about them: a boy comes in wearing his new shoes. Now, for a 13-year-old, an enormous amount of effort would have gone into choosing those shoes. All a guy has to say is 'Nice shoes'—that'll last the boy for a week! Or the way he brushes his hair. Blokes know about that—they've spent inordinate amounts of time as 14-year-olds brushing their hair in the hope some girl will notice them! So 'Your hair's looking good' will do the trick—he's been 'seen'. And remember our 'awesome advice'—don't ever say his hair looks 'awesome', that's just silly.

We encourage our mentors to reflect on what praise they got when they were young and, more importantly, what they didn't get—how did that shape them? What would they have liked? Sometimes it's as simple as showing up to the boy's sports game—and yelling at the ref maybe. This shows the boy he's worth showing up for and says, 'I'm with you.' That's going to mean a lot to any boy—way more than you could imagine. Yeah, he may say it was embarrassing you yelled at the ref but deep inside he loved the fact you were there for him.

If you are struggling to 'find the good', an exercise (much as we hate that word!) we found useful was talking to our kid's subconscious just before we went to sleep. Hold their face in your mind and see the best in them. If there are things you need to tell them that you're struggling with saying, tell them now. It may have had absolutely no impact on our kids whatsoever but somehow it subtly changed how we related to them and that made a difference to their behaviour.

He's doing it

You may or may not know when your boy becomes sexually active, depending on how much of a sharer he is and how attuned you are to him. But we think it's important you do know, because there need to be conversations around contraception and consensual sex.

Neither he nor you want him to be an adolescent father or get a sexually transmitted disease, so making sure he uses protection, regardless of what his sexual partner is using, is really important. He'll need to be adept at and committed to using condoms if he is having sex. These conversations may not be comfortable, but neither is being a teenage dad. So our advice is to bite the bullet—do some research online about how to discuss contraception with your son and just do it. It's probably better if it comes from a trusted man but if there isn't one around, do it yourself, mothers.

We think one really important conversation—possibly the most important one you'll ever have with your boy—is about consensual sex. He needs to make sure that whoever he is having sex with is a willing participant—not someone drugged or drunk or depressed. He needs to know that when girls—or boys—say 'no' they mean 'no'. End of story.

The flawed and damaging mythology that when girls say 'no' they mean 'yes' and that 'she really wants it' is bullshit. Tell your boy he's not going to die from a hard-on—he can go and have a wank. Praise masturbation, because it's gonna save your son's arse! He won't go blind or get hairs on his palms. He will not be smote down by an angry god and he as sure as hell will not become a teenage parent.

Make sure he understands that if he forces himself on someone when he's horny, he'll feel like shit and that person will carry it with them for the rest of their life. New Zealand has an appalling 'rape culture'—make sure your boy isn't part of it.

The good news is that the stats show the majority of young people between 13 and 17 in New Zealand have never had sex. That's 75.6 per cent of the teenage cohort, parents—not bad stats really. The truth is boys are generally quite nervous around people they are attracted to—regardless of their sex—and the gap between boys talking about prowess and conquest and the reality is gaping!

Sexual drive varies widely in men depending on their testosterone levels. Many men say sex wasn't a big deal for them as teenagers, or wasn't as important to them as it was for other boys, and that's congruent with who they are now.

All boys think every other boy is more sexually active than they are, and most men we've interviewed feel shame around being 'late starters'—generally in their late teens or early twenties. They are very relieved to hear they're well within the norm! Which highlights another fact: boys generally don't have very realistic conversations with each other about sex—and that's where parents, or other adults, can step in.

We've already touched on pornography (see 'Let's talk about sex' on page 129), but it's good to reinforce the notion with your boy that pornography is not sex as we commoners know it. It might get his juices going but in reality, sex is physically and emotionally much messier and more complex than how it is depicted in a lot of pornography. He just may not be able to live up to the chiselled, weirdly shaven, Adonis-like creature with a perennial hard-on as seen on *Harry Humps Heidi*. Maybe he won't be able to shag for hours on end and hey, his partner may not want him to! She or he may be looking for a broader expression of intimacy.

This is something you can discuss with your son, from your own experience, if you can find a way in to talk about pornography and its lack of relationship with reality. If you can't, find someone who can. It's become more important these days because porn is as prolific as actual birds and bees.

Finding his sexual compass

One of life's big challenges is working out our sexual orientation. It's the issue that our happiness ultimately hinges on, because going against our orientation will lead to a lack of fulfilment and fractured intimate relationships. As parents, we have a responsibility to both live in our own sexuality authentically and to help our children do the same. It's not always easy, as we face our own fears and prejudices— especially the ones we don't know we have.

Thankfully, in the Western world at least, we have moved past stoning people who are attracted to the same sex. But that's not to say prejudice isn't still alive and well and living in a heart near you. While many of us like to think of ourselves as liberal around sexual orientation and gender identity, it's still a hard road to travel in a largely overtly heterosexual world. Even gay friends of ours struggled to accept their son coming out because they knew the challenges he would potentially face into as a gay man and wanted to spare him that. They also knew it meant the chances of him having children would be narrowed and they mourned the loss of potential grandchildren. Thankfully, that too is easing up as more and more gay couples have children and they have been found to be not just as healthy and happy as kids from heterosexual parents, but even more so!

Social conservatives have been taking pot-shots at LGBT (lesbian, gay, bisexual and transgender) parents forever, but a 2014 Melbourne University study—the largest one ever conducted on non-heterosexual parenting—surveying 315 same-sex parents and 300 children found the only legs conservatives have to stand on are their prejudices. The study reported that in multidimensional measures of child health and wellbeing, the children of gay couples scored about 6 per cent higher than kids in the general population on measures of health and family cohesion. The results line up with previous international research taken on smaller sample sizes.

'It seems that same-sex-parent families and the children in them are getting along well, and this has positive impacts on child health,' lead researcher Simon Crouch told the ABC. He said the study found same-sex parents 'take on roles that are suited to their skill sets rather than falling into those gender stereotypes,' and the result is a 'more harmonious family unit and therefore feeding on to better health and wellbeing.'

We've known lots of kids from LGBT families over many decades and absolutely support the findings of this survey. None of those kids are any more screwed up than our own—they've all faced similar issues throughout their childhoods, adolescence and adult lives and will continue to do so. Let's just put this one to bed, people!

We still absolutely believe that boys need good men in their lives to model off as they stride into manhood—in the same way girls need good women—but being the child of LGBT parents does not preclude these relationships. Our experience is that same-sex parents are generally very comfortable with their kids modelling off good men and women in their wider communities.

Assuming you are on board with your son figuring out his sexual orientation and gender identity, this brief terminology update—with thanks to the Human Rights Campaign—should bring you up to speed and give you a starting point for understanding and facing any sexuality issues your son is having:

- **Sexual orientation:** An inherent or immutable enduring emotional, romantic or sexual attraction to other people.
- **Gender identity:** One's innermost concept of self as male, female, a blend of both or neither—how individuals perceive themselves and what they call themselves. One's gender identity can be the same or different from their assigned sex at birth.
- **Gender expression:** The external appearance of one's gender identity, usually expressed through behaviour, clothing, haircut or voice, and which may or may not conform to socially defined behaviours and characteristics typically associated with being either masculine or feminine.
- **Transgender:** An umbrella term for people whose gender identity and/or expression is different from cultural expectations based on the sex they were assigned at birth. Being transgender does not imply any specific sexual

orientation. Therefore, transgender people may identify as straight, gay, lesbian, bisexual, etc.

- **Gender transition:** The process by which some people strive to more closely align their internal knowledge of gender with its outward appearance. Some people socially transition, whereby they might begin dressing, using names and pronouns and/or be socially recognised as another gender. Others undergo physical transitions in which they modify their bodies through medical interventions.

- **Gender dysphoria:** Clinically significant distress caused when a person's assigned birth gender is not the same as the one with which they identify. According to the American Psychiatric Association's Diagnostic and Statistical Manual of Mental Disorders (DSM), the term— which replaces gender identity disorder—'is intended to better characterise the experiences of affected children, adolescents, and adults'.

That's probably enough homework to be going on with! There is plenty of information available on this subject—don't be afraid to reach out for help early in the piece if you think your son is struggling. We can't stress this enough.

You can kind of see what we are getting at here. It's not your job to decide your son's sexual orientation or gender identity—that's his job—but he will need you right alongside him as he forms his full sexual identity. To be honest, if he is straight, you can breathe a sigh of relief that his sexuality is not another major life issue you need to help him with in a sometimes cruel world, but if he's not, lean into the challenge—he's going to need you.

Drugs and alcohol

Let's lay the bad news out on the table. The reality is kids die on our roads—often because they are under the influence of booze or drugs. And our boys are much more likely to become crash statistics. For the three years 2011–13:

- Of the 269 alcohol- or drug-affected drivers in fatal crashes, 85 per cent were male. Another 28 pedestrians affected by alcohol died.
- For every 100 alcohol- or drug-impaired drivers or riders who died in road crashes, 47 of their passengers and 17 unrelated sober road users died with them.
- On average, there were 67 male drivers and 12 female drivers affected by alcohol or drugs in fatal crashes each year between 2011 and 2013.
- Of all drivers involved in fatal crashes, the 15 to 19 age group is most likely to be affected by alcohol or drugs, closely followed by the 20 to 24 age group.
- Only 14 per cent of female drivers in all fatal crashes were affected by alcohol or drugs compared to 23 per cent of male drivers.
- The difference between the sexes still exists when age and vehicle type are taken into account. For example, of the 20- to 24-year-old car drivers in fatal crashes, 32 per cent of the women and 45 per cent of the men were affected by alcohol or drugs.
- Drivers with restricted or learner licences are more likely to be affected by alcohol or drugs than those with full licences. However, this group falls into the younger age categories, which are associated with more risky driving behaviour overall.

It gets worse:

- Alcohol causes about 1000 deaths in New Zealand every year.
- Thousands more are injured in alcohol-related accidents and assaults.
- More than 120,000 New Zealanders suffer from an alcohol-use disorder.
- Young people, Maori and Pasifika people are especially affected by alcohol-related issues.
- Alcohol is a factor in one-third of all crimes.
- A quarter (25 per cent) of New Zealand drinkers aged 12 to 65 typically drink large amounts when they drink, as do over half (54 per cent) of 18- to 24-year-old drinkers.
- Just over a third of male drinkers aged 18 to 24 get drunk at least once a week.
- The drinking patterns of young people (14 to 18) show a trend towards heavier consumption per occasion.

So there it is; grim reading. As we've said before, there is no shortage of fun-gone-bad stories, and grieving families are sentenced to shattered lives as a result. They don't get to see their beautiful boys grow up to be fine men; they don't get to go to their boys' weddings or cuddle their grandchildren. All because of one night out drinking or drugging. It's a hell of a cost.

What we know about teenagers is that because of the elasticity of their brains, they are much more likely to become addicted to alcohol or drugs than adults. American neurologist and neuroscientist Dr Frances Jensen told Radio New Zealand National that addiction is essentially a form of learning: 'Teenagers are really fast learners—they can learn faster, stronger, harder than adults. Brain cells talk to each other through synapses, which grow when you learn something new. Research shows that the synaptic plasticity—the mouldability of the brain—is much greater in teenagers. The downside is it makes them more vulnerable to addiction—they become addicted faster, stronger, harder than adults.'

But the upside of this fast-learning elasticity is they can change quickly, as they are receptive to good information and stimuli as well. You can build on their quick-learning abilities by giving them concrete information about drugs and alcohol that will hopefully make them stop and think—and help them think through causality. For example, Dr Jensen said studies show that drugs stay longer in teenagers' systems than in adults', 'So I'd tell my sons—"If you smoke pot tonight and have an exam in two days, you're going to do worse. It's a fact."' We'd use the phrase 'medical fact' just to give it more boy-weight.

Or, 'There's a reason why I'm telling you not to smoke dope daily—it will drop your IQ by around 13 to 17 points. Fact.' (As an aside, new research shows IQ is not fixed over a lifetime—in a third of people their IQ goes up, a third down and a third stays the same. There's hope for us yet!)

Unfortunately, your son is likely to be exposed to a lot more substances than we were—and some pretty dangerous ones at that. In our misspent youths (the 1970s) the drugs of choice for our generation (and yes, we did inhale) were dope (cannabis/marijuana), acid (LSD), datura (a hallucinogenic), heroin (an opioid painkiller), cocaine, amphetamine (commonly known as speed or chalk), Mandrax (a sedative and hypnotic, also known as Quaalude), magic mushrooms and booze—mainly beer. We had a number of mind-expanding experiences on various substances and a few not-so-optimal ones that neither of us was keen to repeat. We must have been quick learners. Fortunately, we didn't become addicted to anything and this phase passed without any dramatic effects. And despite dire headline warnings at the time, our children were not born psychotic or with two heads.

So our approach to drug use—including alcohol—is no doubt shaped by our experiences, which were mostly moderate (although there might have been a few very wild nights in there!) and largely positive. We became aware, however, of the negative effects of very early and regular drug use—particularly dope smoking—and by the time our children were teenagers we'd made a decision that we would not glamorise our drug experiences in front of them. Stories of your wild youth might impress your peers but they could prove lethal for your impressionable teenage son! In fact, we said very little about any of our drug escapades until we felt our children were mature enough individuals to hear our stories without being influenced by them.

This strategy worked for us. We know our children have tried various substances themselves but we are confident they do not have any significant issues with drugs. Parenting is often about timing and quantity—finding the right time to tell them and how much.

One of the problems parents face today is the plethora of drugs available to kids now. They are doctored more than the drugs we took, and way more powerful. These include (with thanks to the New Zealand Drug Foundation and TeensHealth):

- **Amphetamines:** Stimulants which speed up functions in the brain and body. They come in pill, tablet or powder form. Amphetamines are usually swallowed, but also can be inhaled or injected.

- **Methamphetamine (P):** A crystal-like powder that is white or off-white, depending on how pure it is. Sometimes it is a small chunk of rock that flakes apart. Meth is swallowed, snorted, smoked or injected. It's the most powerful of the amphetamines.
- **Ketamine:** An anaesthetic which is mostly sold as a white or off-white powder that is snorted. Some people smoke it, often with marijuana or tobacco. It also comes as a liquid that rapists use to spike the drinks of victims.
- **Party pills:** Benzylpiperazine (BZP) party pills are psychoactive substances that have been on the recreational drug scene since around 2000. BZP party pills—now a Class C controlled drug—were designed to mimic the effects of illegal drugs such as methamphetamine, MDMA (ecstasy) and LSD.
- **Anabolic steroids:** Artificially produced hormones that are the same as, or similar to, androgens, the male-type sex hormones. Another group of steroids, sometimes called steroidal supplements, contain dehydroepiandrosterone (DHEA) and/or androstenedione (also known as andro).
- **Ecstasy (also known as E, and more recently Molly):** MDMA is the key ingredient in the drug ecstasy. MDMA is synthetic, meaning it's man-made, and can be cut with other drugs. Most users take it as a pill or capsule.
- **Synthetic cannabinoids:** Chemicals that mimic the effect of THC—one of the ingredients in cannabis.
- **Cough and cold medicines:** There's an ingredient in many over-the-counter cough and cold medicines called dextromethorphan. It's known as DXM for short and its purpose is to suppress the need to cough, but taken in higher doses it creates euphoria.

- **'Study drugs':** Taken to keep students awake, particularly during exam time. Two prescription stimulants are commonly used as 'study drugs': amphetamines like Adderall, Dexedrine or Vyvanse, or methylphenidates like Ritalin or Concerta.

The above list will change as new drugs come on the scene and old ones depart, but you can keep up to date with the help of Google; try searching for 'street drugs' and you'll find lots of information.

The reality is your teenager will be exposed to drugs and alcohol at some stage. He is likely to dabble in some of them and, once again, you are going to have to trust you have built a healthy foundation for exploration in him—while he may play in this space, he won't get lost in it.

But be aware that some of these substances, such as ketamine, can be hugely damaging—lethal even. They can trigger psychotic episodes in teenagers with no history of mental illness. Our mental health inpatient units are full of beautiful young people who dabbled with drugs and literally lost their minds. It's a very long road back from that place.

Our advice is to try to stay close to what your son is experimenting with—find out what he's being offered and research the drugs. Then give him the facts—as simply messaged as you can—and trust some light will go on in the fog of testosterone when he's out there with his mates.

Same with alcohol. We made the decision to socialise our kids around alcohol through having wine on the dinner table and letting them drink at family celebrations. We watched to see what kind of drinkers they were—how much they could handle and how it affected them. Then you've got some information to start talking about responsible drinking. Once again, it's all about being conscious of your own drivers and desires, and communicating with your son so he begins the life journey of understanding his own.

In general, most drugs like alcohol make people happy, calm, confident, alert, chilled out, talkative or want to dance and sing for a short time. If your son is showing signs of paranoia, isolation, anxiety or is just out of touch with reality, then whatever drugs he has taken are destroying him. Get help.

Learning to drive

Don't let his mates teach him how to drive. A girlfriend tried teaching me (Ruth) and I ended up taking out one of the concrete pillars on her parents' two-storey century-old villa! But do be aware that even though you've been on the road for much longer than his mates have, there's still the danger you'll pass on your bad driving habits to your boy. Two of our kids failed their driving tests first time around for driving too fast—obviously something we'd overlooked when teaching them! You don't know what you don't know.

Whoever is the calmest adult driver in your household or whanau is probably the best person to be teaching your boy to drive—otherwise you'll set yourselves up for spectacular meltdowns as heart-stoppingly anxious parent abuses stressed learner driver through gritted teeth, just centimetres from the local supermarket shopping trolley bay. Nerves of steel are required—if that's not you, step away from the car!

If parents aren't up to it, find a good driving instructor. Your local area's Facebook page will have recommendations for someone who is a good fit for your son. This is important, as driving is something he needs to get right—learning to be a good driver from the get-go will hopefully save his life. Because let's be honest here— road crashes are the single biggest killer of 15- to 19-year-olds in New Zealand, and our teen crash rates are among the worst in the developed world.

Teen drivers are most at risk of having a serious crash in the first 6 to 12 months of driving on their own on a restricted licence. In fact, each year there are over 1000 crashes resulting in injury or death involving teen drivers on a restricted licence. Statistically, they are more vulnerable on the road during this period than at any other time in their lives. So make sure he is getting regular driving lessons whilst on his restricted licence; at this stage the instructor will be focusing on hazard awareness, a very good thing for your boy.

Ministry of Transport stats show that in 2014 alone, drivers aged 15 to 24 were involved in 61 fatal crashes, 513 serious injury crashes and 2335 minor injury crashes. Of these crashes, the 15- to 24-year-old drivers had the primary responsibility in 52 of the fatal crashes, 397 of the serious injury crashes and 1771 of the minor injury crashes. These crashes resulted in 58 deaths, 487 serious injuries and 2433 minor injuries.

The total social cost of the crashes in which 15- to 24-year-old drivers were primarily responsible was $718 million—22 per cent of the social cost associated with all injury crashes. That's one hell of a cost.

After alcohol, losing control and excessive speed are the other major contributing factors for young drivers involved in fatal crashes. Over half (55 per cent) of the young drivers involved in fatal crashes had alcohol and/or drugs and/or speed identified as factors contributing to the crash. Young drivers are more than twice as likely to have speed or alcohol as a factor than drivers over the age of 25.

Given these appalling outcomes for our young male drivers, we think something drastic needs to happen around driver training in this country. It may be that our model needs changing to something more akin to some intensive European driver training systems, in which young drivers attend week-long driving schools that include driving skills in hazardous conditions, how to maintain their vehicle and defensive driving.

The minimum age to apply for a full licence in Sweden is 18, and applicants usually sit around 13 or 14 tests before they are ready for the final test. Then they get a full licence that carries a probationary period of two years, during which time the licence can be revoked if the person commits a serious traffic offence, in which case they have to re-sit it.

New Zealand Transport Agency has a great website, safeteendriver.co.nz, with lots of practical tips on teaching your son to drive, how to choose a car for him, learner licence restrictions and much more. You can also check out psychologist Nigel Latta's 'Surviving Teen Driving' YouTube video series for more info on teaching your boy to drive.

Social media and gaming

Our kids are spending more and more time on devices and we need to know what they are doing on them. The good news is, it's not all bad! Despite the prophets of doom condemning gamers to a life of anti-social isolation, recent German studies have come in on the positive side of gaming. Apparently the hippocampus—involved in spatial navigation—grows during gaming, as players use this part of the brain to navigate a virtual world. In one study, the cerebellum—an area of the brain involved in coordinating fine-motor skills—showed growth, and the right prefrontal cortex grew. This is the part of the brain involved in planning and organisation—important skills for games like Super Mario 64.

Dr Dayna Galloway—a lecturer at the School of Arts, Media and Computer Games at Abertay University in the UK—said in a BBC iWonder article that as well as skills related to these areas of brain growth, playing video games can bring other benefits, including the ability to think in three dimensions, and even improving our eyesight.

'Some studies have shown that first-person shooter games improve a player's capacity to think about objects in three dimensions,' said Dr Galloway. His research shows that medics who played video games were instinctively better at keyhole surgery, and a Dutch surgeon has now developed a game designed to train doctors in this specialised technique.

We've had first-hand experience of this. We watched friends of ours agonise over their son's addiction to gaming for some five years. He was up all hours of the night playing international teams, ate erratically, became an uncommunicative sloth, put on weight and was very demotivated. Then he hit his mid-twenties and announced he was going to become a plastic surgeon! He took himself off to medical school and is now focused on his career. So there you go; maybe he was simply gaining the skills he would require later.

Dr Galloway said another unexpected bonus of gaming is improved eyesight. One study of first-person shooters showed an improvement in their 'contrast sensitivity function'—the ability to make out subtle changes in image brightness. The study also found that focusing on a screen to aim at the bad guy exercised our eyes, possibly helping to maintain visual acuity over time. But let's be honest—the world of gaming can also really isolate boys, keeping them from real-life interactions and relationships. 'It can be a fantasy world that supports violence and objectifies women,' says Big Buddy programme manager Steve Sobota. 'Practically, it also keeps them from being active and engaged with their body and their physical environment—from nature. Boys need that.'

Same with too much social media. (Well . . . same with too much of anything, really!) If your teen is spending countless hours trolling social media for signs of life instead of living one, it's time to set some boundaries. Maybe think about South Korea, where they have recently set up 12-day digital detox boot-camps in remote mountain areas for kids addicted to their online lives. Described as having had 'lost childhoods', some of these kids had never had a 'real' friend—only virtual ones—and needed to go back to socialisation 101! We can believe this—a music teacher friend says his intermediate school students 'chat' via social media in the classroom rather than talking to each other! What's that about?!

Fortunately, there is lots of great advice on the digital space available to parents now. Vodafone's Digi-Parenting site is well worth a look, as is NetSafe. You can find lots of great info on how families can stay connected in the digital space and how to keep your kids (and yourself!) safe.

The thing to really watch out for is cyber-bullying, which can have devastating effects—particularly on adolescents. (See 'Suicide and mental illness' on page 187.)

It's ultimately about negotiating a balance of physical and mental activity—of online and face-to-face communication. Remember, you're not powerless to control online use—you still make the rules for now, and if your teen is doing something you think is really dangerous and they won't listen to your concerns, pull the plug until they will listen! Sure they'll sulk and act out—just another day in teenage paradise! When they're ready to talk they're back online.

Suicide and mental illness

There's no denying New Zealand youth mental health and suicide rates are grim—we have the second highest rate of youth suicide in the OECD. Being young, male, brown and poor puts youth (15- to 24-year-olds) at greatest risk. Something is going very, very wrong for boys in the land lauded as the greatest country on earth to raise kids.

The only positive news is that provisional youth suicide numbers in 2013–14 were down on the previous year, with 113 suicides compared with 144 in 2012–13. Of these, 35 young men aged 15 to 19, and 44 aged 20 to 24 took their own lives. Seventeen young women in each age group suicided. This was the lowest number of suicides in people aged 15 to 19 since coronial records began in 2007–08.

But while Ministry of Health stats boast the overall suicide rate has dropped by 29.8 per cent from a peak in 1998, and a drop has been seen in many age groups, some people still remain at higher risk—and our young men are among them. The suicide rate is 3.5 times higher in men than in women, and it is highest among young people aged 15 to 24 (19.3 deaths per 100,000). As mentioned above, Maori and people living in low socio-economic areas are also over-represented in the statistics.

Add to that youth accounting for 34.7 per cent (1052) of all intentional self-harm hospitalisations in 2012. It's the only area where girls outnumber boys, by approximately 50 per cent.

The slippery slope to mental illness and possible suicide starts early: around 33,000 children (4 per cent of children aged 2 to 14) were diagnosed with emotional and behavioural problems in 2012–13. Boys were almost twice as likely to have been diagnosed with emotional and behavioural problems as girls, and boys aged 10 to 14 had the highest rate of diagnosed problems, with a whopping 1 in 10 affected.

These kids won't necessarily funnel directly into the mental health system but a good number of them will, and our advice is to get as much support for them when they are young as you possibly can. Identifying issues now—including any learning difficulties associated with ADHD, dyslexia, dyspraxia, foetal alcohol spectrum disorder, etc.—will save a lot of pain later.

Dr Frances Jensen told Radio New Zealand National that high rates of youth mental illness are tied into development of the teenage brain. 'Most mental illness—depression, bipolar, schizophrenia—comes on in the late teens, early twenties—that's when it manifests.' The frontal lobes have to be largely developed to manifest these diseases, Jensen said, and parents have to be vigilant during these years. Her recommendation for parents? Talk to the school counsellor or doctor if their son is more than usually moody or has appetite issues, his personal hygiene is going down, or he is losing friends.

We wonder what it is about New Zealand culture that puts our teenagers—particularly our boys—at such great risk of suicide. What are we missing about them, and what needs to happen to stop them seeing suicide as a way out of their dark places?

One explanation for our high suicide rate may lie in our ancestry. As a relatively new nation, our men have suffered over two centuries of dislocation that has left them struggling to form a male identity—separated from the fathers, grandfathers, uncles and wider whanau who would have mentored them into manhood.

Maori men lost connection to their communities over decades of conflict with pakeha colonisers and then suffered huge loss of life during the two world wars—World War I (1914–18) and II (1939–45). Add to that the mass urban migrations of the 1950s and 1960s: in 1956, 76 per cent of Maori lived in rural areas; by 1976, 78 per cent lived in urban areas. As Jade Reidy wrote in *West: The History of Waitakere*, 'Severed from traditional whanau links, they found themselves at sea with unfamiliar mortgage payments to meet, budgeting, and the temptation of the local pub. Many were school leavers and solo mums.'

Reidy notes that by around 1970, 'nearly two-thirds of the housing mortgages administered by Maori Affairs were in arrears. The department was inundated with Maori who had lost their jobs, had no money or food and nowhere to stay. By the mid-1970s the children of this first generation of urban Maori were forming gangs as a result of the breakdown of whanau links.'

Pasifika people—mainly Samoans—didn't fare much better when they were encouraged to emigrate to people our factories in the early 1960s.

European settlers also experienced dislocation from their male mentors as they sailed across the globe to pastures new from the mid-1800s. This was a double-edged sword—it provided men with the opportunity to break with rigid social structures that limited their life choices, but it also left them isolated from their communities, adrift from the older men in their lives who would have helped shape their male psyches and given them a sense of place.

(Not necessarily all good, granted, but a sense of connectedness and belonging nonetheless.) Instead, these immigrant men had to carve out their sense of what it was to be a man through hard physical graft and becoming jacks of all trades, men alone who could turn their hands to anything and everything. The upside is this lifestyle created a trait of entrepreneurship for which New Zealand is famous; the downside is that without good mentors, our men became desensitised, insular and self-contained—men struggling with emotional intelligence.

And this, we believe, lies somewhere at the core of our high male suicide rates. It's time we talked more about this connection between emotional intelligence and suicide. It's time men practised and modelled more self-reflection and encouraged the boys in their lives to talk about stuff that matters. It's time we acknowledged how sensitive boys and men are, and that they need tools to deal with this, in the same way they need tools to fix things.

It's encouraging to see younger generations of men coming through now who are much more emotionally articulate and able to share emotions with people other than their partners or wives—an Achilles' heel if anything happens to that person and probably why older New Zealand men are also so at risk of suicide (in fact, that's a growing statistic).

In terms of what we can do to help our boys feel connected and encourage them to share more, UN advisor Professor Robert Blum, a global expert on teenage health, has some really simple advice for parents: eating one family meal a day together is key to staying connected with your kids. 'Talk to your kids, talk to them, talk to them, talk to them and when you don't believe they are listening keep talking, because they are.' Hear, hear!

Body image issues

Boys now face the same pressure as girls to 'look right'. And for boys growing up in the 21st century, that means sporting six-pack abs and chiselled pecs! The fat-free, sculptured image is pervasive. According to the 2011 Pacific Obesity Prevention in Communities study, 56 per cent of adolescent males reported being unhappy with their weight, and two in five are actively trying to shed kilos. In Australia, body image is consistently named as one of the top three concerns for young men.

Current ab'd-up body images are supported by action figures that reinforce unrealistic body targets for boys. Dr Raymond Lemberg, an American clinical psychologist and an expert on male eating disorders, told *The Atlantic* magazine that action figures are the male equivalent of Barbie dolls in terms of unrealistic body images. 'We're presenting men in a way that is unnatural. In the last decade or two, action figures have lost a tremendous proportion of fat and added a substantial proportion of muscle, But only 1 or 2 per cent of [males] actually have that body type.'

The danger lies in the other 98 per cent of young men trying to achieve this unrealistic body shape. It's created a wave of what's known as 'muscle dysmorphia'—the male equivalent of anorexia and just as dangerous. The hallmarks are compulsive exercise, an obsession with diet, including food restrictions, and at the worst end of it, taking steroids and peptides to help build muscle. Depression, rage attacks and suicidal tendencies have all been linked to long-term steroid use. Because adolescents are experiencing major growth, they are particularly vulnerable to the negative effects of steroids.

Our advice is unequivocal on this one: if you are worried that your boy's interest in his appearance has become obsessive or unhealthy, get help. Talk to your doctor; seek advice from a specialist in eating disorders. The quicker you catch it, the better.

> ## What to look out for
>
> - Compulsive exercising.
> - Obsession with diet, including food restrictions.
> - Mood swings.
> - Detachment from friends.
> - Not wanting to eat with other people.
> - Changes in size and shape.
> - Interest in and/or taking steroids and peptides to help build muscle.

Reaching out for help

Remember, reaching out for help is not a weakness; it's simply an indication that you haven't yet stumbled upon the info you need to help or support your boy with whatever is troubling you and/or him currently. You wouldn't think twice about seeking medical advice or treatment if you thought he'd broken his leg—same deal if you think something's coming unstuck for him emotionally and you simply don't know what to do.

Getting some input from someone you trust—maybe an older man you admire—makes a lot more sense than both you and your son floundering around in the mud, hoping things will 'come right' through osmosis. That's a risky game—sometimes it works, sometimes it doesn't, depending on the problem. This is the same for women raising boys alone—reach out to men you respect and listen to their advice. The onset of the nuclear family is relatively recent in human history and has its limitations; ask someone in your 'village' to help if you need to. You may be pleasantly surprised when they tell you they feel honoured to have been approached.

At Big Buddy, we get asked by a lot of solo mums, as well as by people in our extended social circles, for advice on getting their sons and grandsons through tough patches. We always try to fully engage in these conversations because we believe we have a collective responsibility to our boys—to mentor them into healthy manhood.

Here are some of the most common problems we hear and our responses to them:

- **My boy spends all his time in his room and doesn't want to socialise with the family.** We ask further questions to establish how widespread this is, e.g. if he is isolating from his peers as well—a key alarm bell. If not, then it could be a natural phase of moving away from his parents—particularly his mum. This sort of isolation is fairly normal and not uncommon—it's his way of separating himself from adults and forming his own social identity. Usually his peer relationships deepen during this time. Just stay close to him as best you can and trust the foundations you have laid down with him.

- **He's separating from his peers as well.** This needs to be addressed—talk to him; talk to his friends and teachers about how they are finding him. Don't shame him but do your best to bring him out into the light of social contact. If nothing you try works, take action and get a counsellor involved.

- **He's smoking dope.** This natural separation phase combined with dope can be really problematic—dangerous even, depending on his reaction to dope. Most boys get chilled out and relaxed on it but some kids, in our experience, can get very paranoid and edge into mental-health issues territory. If you think your boy is smoking dope or, worse still, synthetic cannabis, which is really edgy, and you think it's a problem, get help. As we've said, do your research on it and give him the facts straight.

- **I think my boy is reading bad stuff on the internet.** We advise talking to NetSafe about how to get your/his computer shielded from really bad sites. But try talking to him about what he is reading as well—it's good if Dad or another trusted man can do this.

- **My boy is hanging out with the bad boys at school and getting into trouble now, when he was never like this.** Hopefully you have done some of the background relationship work we talked about earlier, and can have this conversation as it happens and understand his motivations. If you think the 'bad boy' influence is going to persist and end up being really harmful to your boy, don't muck around—change schools. If the influence is in the neighbourhood, consider moving neighbourhoods (seriously) or consider sending him away to a relative for a while. We did this once with one of our kids who was teetering on the edge of a bad situation and—in our then unwanted opinion— compromising her future, so we sent her to stay with relatives on the other side of the world for a few months. It opened her mind and sent her in a whole new direction.

- **My boy is not interested in school anymore and I am worried about his future.** Schools don't always work for boys. (See 'Secondary school and university—making good decisions' on page 159.) Consider moving teachers or schools—it may help if he finds a brilliant but rare motivational teacher! The goal is, of course, to get him through to the minimal school qualification at the very least if you can, but after that maybe a break from education is not a bad thing. Many of our mentors did that and later, after the turbulent teenage years, got back into it, but with very different attitudes—they were far more motivated after having worked in a supermarket or fast-food outlet for a couple of years!

- **My boy seems really unmotivated about finding a job or pursuing further education.** Encourage him to volunteer for something bigger than himself—eco stuff, the local zoo, a hospice shop—anywhere he can help others. Get him out of his room and into the world!

- **My boy wants to know the truth about his father.** The truth could be as hard as the father suicided or was a rapist, or the boy simply hasn't been told much about his dad, who disappeared at some stage. If he is 14-plus and is ready—i.e. has asked a few times—take time to sit with him and tell him the full story; not the 'truth' necessarily but your story about his dad. Our advice is to refrain from loading too much emotional content into the story—keep it really factual. He may want to know more later and you can work out what support he may need to hear very painful information.

- **What if his father suicided and the boy doesn't know?** This news is generally very hard for a boy to handle, so you need to be sure he is ready to hear it. We suggest engaging a counsellor to help. Research shows that boys of suicided fathers can really struggle to come to terms with the perception that the main guy in his man-tribe did not care for him enough to stay alive. He will need ongoing support, e.g. checking in with him regularly after he hears this news.
- **My boy has stuck a knife in his bedroom door.** He needs to see a counsellor and you need to do whatever you need to get him to one. Bribery, coercion and corruption are all good. It may be you need to go together—he may have things he needs to say to you that are better said with a mediating presence.

We want to stress here that counselling is really important if boys are becoming increasingly depressed, aggressive or isolated. Look for a good male counsellor if possible, but we also know of boys who have worked very well with great female counsellors. Ask your doctor for a referral and find out what financial support is available if you need it.

It's a good idea to introduce the idea of seeing a counsellor before the turbulent teens, so he may be less resistant to the idea when it really matters. Also tell him why you saw a counsellor—or his dad did, or your brother—to normalise it. Learning to reflect on and process what happens in his life will bode well for later—if or when he comes unstuck at other times, e.g. relationship or marriage problems, children, career issues, etc. Our experience is counsellors don't always get it right—in fact, some of them are crap—but keep going till you find a good one who works in a way that suits you—they are worth their weight in gold.

Summary

Somehow—through grace and stumbling good management—you are surviving the minefield of the teenage years. Well done, you! The themes we've explored in this chapter are:

- The teenage years are a wild ride.
- Testosterone levels peak during these years.
- His body clock has changed.
- His brain develops much later than his body.
- He's up for much more adventure and will take risks.
- Fun can turn bad.
- He has heightened emotions.
- You need to stay connected to him—you need face-to-face time, to eat meals together.
- He needs more time alone to think and process.
- He needs to walk the 'bridge of adolescence'—to break away from you.
- You need to know your own drivers and address your own issues to effectively parent him.
- Look at who he is and how he thrives before making secondary school and university decisions.
- He's probably going to be *very* irritating at times.
- You'll need to dig deep to see the good in him.
- Talk to him about consensual sex.
- Support him to figure out his sexual orientation.
- His alcohol and drug use need management.

- Make sure he learns to drive well.
- As with anything, social media and gaming is OK in moderation.
- You need to manage his risk around mental illness and suicide.
- Stay alert to his body-image issues.
- Reach out for help if you need it.

There's a lot going on during these years and it's going to take every ounce of patience you can muster to stay close to your son and help him navigate these stormy seas. The great thing is that, just like a chrysalis, with your help he'll emerge into a gorgeous man who will do you proud.

Keep that in mind, along with the words of Dr Frances Jensen: *'Teenagers are fast learners—they learn quicker, faster and harder than adults.* Your secret weapon is knowing your boy is just as receptive to good information and stimuli as he is to bad.'

Make sure you build on his talent for quick learning by putting researchable facts about topics like drugs and alcohol in front of him. Hopefully, he'll stop and think before he acts—will weigh up choices and consequences, and make the right call. Not every time, but often enough to help him survive 'the wild ride'.

Go well, fellow hormone warriors—may the force be with you!

Activities for youth

- Support your boy to enrol in a youth programme like Scouts or surf lifesaving.
- Cook meals and eat together—try out recipes from different countries.

- Attend a local government meeting or planning session.
- Teach your boy how to legally download material off the internet.
- Teach him about cyber safety.
- Teach him about internet banking.
- Plan a budget and teach him how to do a cashflow and check his online balance.
- Fill out a job application and teach him about job interviews, what to say, do and ask.
- Attend a court hearing—small claims, driving offence charges, etc.
- Begin to learn the road code, how to drive a car, how to change a tyre, how to back a trailer.
- Go tramping—stay overnight in huts or tents.
- Go to concerts—listen to music together; find out what he likes and why.
- Play golf.
- Go mountain biking.
- Try a new sport.
- If you're fixing something at home, let him help.
- Learn a language together.
- Go for walks together.
- Check out your ancestry online.
- Ask him to help you build/renovate/fix something.

FIVE

Go west, young man: 18-plus

Try not to become a man of success, but rather try to become a man of value.

Albert Einstein

By the time your boy turns 18 a lot of your work is done. You're effectively just walking alongside him now as he strides into manhood, trusting all the good stuff you've poured into and around him will see him through; hoping he will be happy and live a useful, fulfilling life; believing that the risks you've allowed and encouraged him to take will enable him to make good decisions and that luck will be on his side.

He is probably either still finishing Year 13, studying at tertiary level, doing an apprenticeship, out working or a NEET—a young person aged 15 to 24 who is 'Not in Education, Employment or Training'—a situation you will both find very challenging. (See 'He's NEET' on page 206.)

By now you'll be getting more and more glimpses of the man your boy is becoming—what his interests are; what his dress style is; who he's attracted to; the sorts of girlfriends/boyfriends he chooses; what type of career path he's aiming for or heading down. He's probably starting to make noises about going flatting—just be aware that he may boomerang in and out of home again up until his mid- to late twenties, when his life (and income) begins to settle. The good news is they usually fly back in for only a few months before heading off on their next adventure. It's actually pretty easy to enjoy them during this phase!

But a word of warning here—you may want to wear protective clothing when you visit his flat! Boys-only flats are the worst we've seen, with many of them featuring layers of unidentifiable filth that even rats would turn their noses up at. If your boy lives in one of these, make sure he takes the washing bag he will bring home directly to the laundry and quarantine it there until you are sure it's vermin-free. Oh yes, and your son will likely be spotty with pimples as his diet deteriorates, and tired from too many late nights and over-indulgence in all the booze and/or dope he wasn't allowed to consume at home. The good news is this stage will pass! He'll get sick of living in a pigsty and tidy up his act eventually—just wait it out.

Sometime after I (Ruth) first went flatting at 16 with a bunch of miscreants whose main goal in life was to avoid work at all costs (this was the 1970s, remember), I went to the doctor complaining of chronic fatigue. He asked me questions about my lifestyle, and having established that I was unemployed by choice and living on milk stolen from neighbours' letterboxes and whatever else I could ferret from the bins at the local Chinese restaurant, he told me I had mild malnutrition, was the laziest person he had ever met and to get out of his office! Maybe he forgot the part in the Hippocratic oath he signed that said: 'With regard to healing the sick, I will devise and order for them the best diet, according to my judgment and means; and I will take care that they suffer no hurt or damage.' Nah—really, he did me a favour. After we'd all stopped rolling about the floor laughing at him, we sort of cleaned up our acts some and joined the grown-ups.

Of course, some boys never leave home. They are the Peter Pans of this world—often with 'Italian mammas'—who never quite grow up and leave the family nest (interestingly, one in three Italian men sees his mother every day and seven out of ten unmarried Italian men over the age of 35 live with their parents!). We'd have to say we don't see this as optimal in the trajectory of a man's life—gaining independence from your parents is a healthy path to travel, particularly necessary when it comes time to be a partner and father yourself. That's not to say young men should disassociate completely from their mums and dads—just that they need to separate from them emotionally and physically to form their own identity and make the shift from boy to man.

Making the separation happen is a sometimes delicate dance of push-pull. Sometimes our boys may need a push—and it might not be a gentle one—and sometimes we parents need to let go as they pull away: it may hurt, but unless your son has major health issues, he needs to get out there into the world and into his life by his early twenties.

Your son will go through a lot of changes as he moves into manhood. Remember, his frontal cortex isn't fully developed until his mid-twenties, so he's probably still doing some stuff that looks damned stupid and downright dangerous to you.

He'll make decisions that flummox you. Our son, having left school in what was then the fifth form (Year 11) due to a number of factors, had good technical skills and eventually got a job with Wang, then a leading computer company. He was living back at home at this time, and off he'd trotted to work each day in his smart shirt and tie. Sorted, we thought, having worried ourselves sick about his future. But no. He came home from work one day and said, 'I'm sorry, Dad, but I can't do this. It's not me. I want to go snowboarding in Canada with my mates.' Really? (Well, we actually said a lot more than that—some of it not particularly kind!)

But he taught us a really important lesson as parents, and that's that we can't plan our kids' destinies—they belong to them. Our son followed his impulse to hoon off snowboarding and eventually washed up in northern Japan, where he now runs a chain of snowboard shops employing over 120 staff! And he found the gorgeous girl he would marry and settle down with. Somehow he knew what he needed to do to get to where he was going and we just had to learn to trust him.

Consequently, we bought all our kids a backpack when they turned 21! It was our way of saying, 'You have our blessing to go off and explore the world. To create your own lives. To have fun. We trust you to do that.' And it worked out really well. They are well-travelled adults who have had lots of risky adventures and, fortunately, lived to tell their tales.

(By the way, it's worth knowing that while getting knocks to the head—an injury parents often fear most—in the course of taking risks isn't optimal or desirable, fortunately neuroscience is weighing in on the positive side of brain plasticity. Everything from therapy and brain training to diet and exercise . . . there are myriad ways to retrain the brain to reorganise itself throughout life by forming new neural connections, according to American psychiatrist and brain-disorder specialist Dr Daniel Amen. Dr Amen says in his TEDx lecture 'The most important lesson from 83,000 brain scans' the brain can form new neural pathways that can repair damage and compensate for injury. Once the brain repairs, people make different and better decisions, he says. Thank goodness for that!)

We think having a 'gap year'—or three—between school and tertiary study is a good idea. It gives young people time to blow out some education cobwebs and get a clearer picture of what they want to study or do with their lives, as opposed to just falling into a degree, often chosen by well-meaning parents. Our experience is that when they do choose to study later, they are more focused—there's a ripeness about them that augers well for their careers.

One of our daughters worked at a number of different jobs before deciding at 26 to return to New Zealand and do a communications degree. She's now at the top of her profession, working very successfully in high-level communications. Her partner was a builder who decided to study architecture in his late thirties. He was super-focused when studying and is now loving working for a well-respected architecture firm. So don't be scared if they take time out from study or training— trust they'll come back to it when their time is right.

Fortunately, there are lots of great ways to stay in touch with your boy when he's out exploring the world—Skype, social media, etc.— but don't overpower him with your own needs. While you may seek reassurance that he's safe and happy, he needs to learn he can take risks and survive on his own, and you need to trust he'll ask for your help if he needs it. He will be pretty wrapped up in himself and his adventures, so don't feel too hurt if he doesn't communicate back to the parent ship very often—it's part of the process. There will be the odd call asking for financial support but hopefully it wanes over time as he becomes self-supporting. (See 'He's all grown up' on page 209.)

Sometimes you'll watch him choose partners about whom every cell in your body screams '*beware!*'. All you can do is stay connected to him however you can and be there when/if he needs you. But do look out for loss of confidence, lack of energy, depression and/or anxiety, and if you are seriously worried the relationship is messing with your boy's head, talk to him about your fears, naming them as your own, but checking if they have any validity. Once again, trust you've got enough relationship money in the bank for him to tell you if he's in real trouble.

And another thing—if he breaks up with his partner, don't diss his ex (not to him, anyway!). Exes have a habit of bouncing back and before you know it, there they are, sitting across from you at Christmas dinner! Know that just as your child found a way back to their partner, so you will too—just give it time and plenty of goodwill. Put aside all the grumbles you listened to when your son and his partner were in their darkest hour and start again. Try to see all the great qualities he sees in his partner and focus on those instead of carrying grudges he no longer holds. If you can't move on, it's guaranteed you'll see less of your boy. And if the relationship goes sour again, trust he'll talk to you if he needs support.

Now your big boy's got a life, it's about finding time to still do the things you enjoy together, and to look for new ways to engage with him. There's no doubt it's harder and there's some grief involved in letting him go, but his waning interest in you isn't a reflection on you—in fact, it's an affirmation you've done your job well, as he goes out into the world and starts mapping his own course. Well done, you!

Finally, a quote from a friend's adult son, in response to her 'banging on' about how he was packing his suitcase as he prepared to travel overseas: 'Twenty-five, Mum—not five.' Says it all, really.

Maybe the challenge here—especially if your last child is leaving home—is to re-evaluate your life and start carving out a future that isn't centred on child-rearing. Grandchildren will come in time and that's way fun—all love and not nearly as much responsibility!

He's NEET

This is a growing phenomenon, with the NEET (Not in Employment, Education or Training) rate for young people estimated at 15 per cent in May 2015—more than double the overall unemployment rate of 5.8 per cent. According to Statistics New Zealand, that meant about 64,000 young people were out of work, despite many of them being educated and motivated.

While youth unemployment rates have fallen from a peak of 20 per cent following the global financial crisis (2007–08), many young people are still battling with the mental health challenges that go hand in hand with unemployment, as well as government policies that make getting a foot in the job market a real struggle.

Kiwi digital journalist Mava Moayyed, who was unemployed for approximately seven months in 2014, says in online publication *The Wireless*: '. . . research into the effects of joblessness on young people paints a grim picture, and a New Zealand study shows long-term unemployed youth have a heightened risk of criminal offending, substance abuse, suicide and homelessness. A UK study revealed at least 40 per cent of jobless young people faced mental illness as a direct result of unemployment.'

This is supported by research by the UN's International Labor Organization (ILO), which reported, 'Increased crime rates in some countries, increased drug use, moving back home with the parents, depression—all of these are common consequences for a generation of youth that, at best, has become disheartened about the future, and, at worst, has become angry and violent.'

A grim picture indeed. But there is a lot parents can do to support their NEET boys to help them hold onto their sense of self-worth and purpose during these challenging times. We suggest you:

- Keep up the regular family meals so he stays connected.
- Make sure your son's CV is current and sharp.
- Help him write cover letters for job applications.
- Check out his Facebook page and maybe help him clean it up—lots of employers look at them now.
- Make sure his mobile message is articulate.
- Work your contacts—remember, a lot of job opportunities come via word of mouth.
- Find out if he's entitled to any government support, e.g. a Jobseeker Support payment, while he's looking for a job.
- Encourage him to stay healthy by maintaining a good diet and exercising daily—run, walk or go to the gym with him if necessary.
- Suggest he volunteers somewhere—anywhere. Help him find social services in your community that need support. Remind your boy that the more active he is in the world, the more likely he is to get a job.
- Send your boy to a relative or friend if they need help at home or at work—the more skills he gains, the better.

- Explore him doing a mindfulness course or something similar to help keep his spirits up and stay focused on the 'now' so he doesn't slip into depression.
- Remind him daily that the only constant thing in life is change and that this period will pass. He will get work—he does have a future.
- Praise him for the small things.
- Hug him often.

Your job is to try to look past how incredibly annoying it is watching him laze around feeling sorry for himself when you have work coming out your ears and keep putting possibilities in front of him. He'll scoff at them and reject most of them out of hand, but just occasionally they'll find a crack in his negative persona and, as Leonard Cohen so poignantly reminds us that's where the light gets in. Keep trying until something grabs your beautiful boy's imagination, and watch him fly!

This is a time for watchful patience. If your son is in the NEET limbo by choice, maybe he is trying to find his own way forward by stopping first. He may need time to flounder around a little before moving forward. When tracking dogs lose the scent they run around in seemingly chaotic circles until finally one finds the scent and the whole pack launches off in a new direction. Your son may be in that position.

If you see indecision, new ideas that come and go, vacantly staring at nothing, these are all good signs—but if you see dullness, long periods alone and/or no interest in new ideas, then he's dropped out of productive floundering into early depression and will need help.

He's all grown up

We've talked some about staying connected to your adult son and we'd like to offer a few more thoughts on this. The truth is, it's often harder to stay connected with sons than daughters because generally speaking, girls are more relational than boys. Some boys are relational, of course, and that certainly helps when it comes to staying in touch, but our personal experience is it's harder to maintain close contact with sons, particularly when they live overseas and lead very busy lives. Our relationships were likely also more challenging because we were a 'blended' family, with quite a bit of emotional baggage to overcome.

Regardless, we used to beat ourselves up about not making enough regular contact with our son and his wife, who have lived mostly in Japan for well over a decade. But it was pointless—despite our good intentions to Skype more, etc., we all got busy again and before we knew it we were back to the same old pattern of either feeling guilty about not making enough contact with him or shitty at him for not trying harder. A beat-up going nowhere!

What we decided was to let him and us off the hook and take a different approach—to drop all the guilt and expectations, and accept the situation as it is. It doesn't mean we love our son any less because the contact is not as regular as it is with our girls (who all live in New Zealand). It just means we are free to really enjoy each other when we do see him and his wife because we've kicked guilt and blame into touch!

So, what we've found works best for us is making sure the time we do spend together is quality time—we set aside time to fully engage with our son and his wife when they come home to New Zealand for a holiday, respecting that they also have other family commitments. And what we find is that even though there may not have been a huge amount of communication in the intervening months or sometimes even a couple of years between visits, our son is fully present when he is with us. He's hungry for family and we bask in having him around. This is when we catch up on where he's at and share lots of family stories that have been missed out on. He gets to bed back into the family and deepen his sense of place. When they leave again it's always sad but life goes on and we all really look forward to the next visit.

There's no doubt boys change as they become men. For one, their testosterone levels peak at around that age of 17 to 18 and continue to be high until they begin to decline by about 1 per cent per year after the age of 30. As these and other hormonal changes occur, so too will your relationship with him change. In fact, you may witness him morphing into the emotional pragmatist his father is/was! Don't be surprised by this—it seems there is a perfectly good explanation.

Until recently, differences between how women and men feel and express emotions were put down to nurture—how we were raised. In *The Male Brain,* American neuropsychiatrist Dr Louann Brizendine writes that how parents raise children can reinforce or suppress parts of our basic biology, but we now know the emotional processing is different in male and female brains. 'Research has suggested that our brains have two emotional systems that work simultaneously: the mirror-neuron system or MNS, and the temporal-parietal junction system, or TPJ. Males seem to use one system more, and females seem to use the other more.'

MNS controls emotional empathy, while TPJ controls analysis and is solution-focused. You're getting the picture here about who uses which system by now, eh? 'The male brain is able to use the TPJ starting in late childhood, but after puberty a male's reproductive hormones may cement a preference for it,' writes Dr Brizendine. 'Researchers have found that the TPJ keeps a firm boundary between emotions of the "self" and "other". This prevents men's thought processes from being infected by other people's emotions, which strengthens their ability to cognitively and analytically find a solution.'

(Note to women: when you wail at the man in your life, 'Why can't you just listen to me?' or 'Why do you have to try to fix everything?', you now know why he can't.)

As an adult, your son is not looking for advice in the same way he may have previously, and he'll expect his decisions to be respected. But he still needs and loves you, and staying connected to him is just as important as it ever was.

Dr Jeffrey Jensen Arnett, a research professor in the department of psychology at Clark University, Massachusetts, says in a *Bottom Line Personal* article that much of the angst between parents and adult children stems from the tug-of-war over whose life it is. 'There often is a disconnect between parents who still want to shape their grown-up kids' future course and the kids who are determined to live their lives their own way.'

Here's our advice to parents wanting to stay close to their adult son (which we have not always successfully followed!), with thanks to Dr Arnett:

- **Don't use money to control your adult son.** If you're offering financial support to him you can set ground rules about how that money is used, but you can't use it to control other aspects of his life.

- **Don't push your son to take a job in a field that pays well but that he doesn't like.** Not only might he hold his unhappiness against you, his lack of enthusiasm could inhibit his career growth.
- **Make him welcome at home if he needs to come back for a while.** Many adult children come home for a short time. Almost always, their return is temporary because they prefer to live independently as soon as they can afford to do so.
- **Try not to ask probing questions about his life**. If he wants to share something personal, he will. Just make sure you have the time and space for him to share stuff if he does want to.
- **Don't overdo the contact.** It may be cheap and easy to stay in contact these days but that doesn't mean you have to do it all the time. Follow your son's lead on how much is too much—you'll get a good feel for frequency and length of time as you go along.
- **Don't overlook your adult son's romantic partner at family get-togethers.** Be sure to include your son's partner in family gatherings and try to make him/her feel welcome and comfortable. As we said earlier, the more comfortable your grown son's partner is with you, the more likely you are to see more of your son!
- **Ask him if he wants your advice before you impart your wisdom.** The odds of a negative reaction decline greatly if you ask your son if he would like your input before you offer it. Warning: respect his response. If he says he prefers to work through the problem on his own, keep your advice to yourself.

Now is the time to savour your grown son—to admire the man he has grown into. You can congratulate yourself for some of this and feel gratitude to all the other significant people in his life who put time and energy into him. You'll get to enjoy his successes and he'll likely still need a shoulder to lean and/or cry on from time to time. He'll come unstuck for sure occasionally and will need to know you're there. But what he'll need most from you now is to know you are getting on with your own life—that you still love and care for him, but that you are not needing to live through him. The last thing he needs now is to feel responsible for you, because he's busy making other plans.

Summary

So your boy is well on the road to becoming a man. You are probably feeling a mixture of exhilaration, fear, pride and love as he readies himself to be out in the world away from your protective wings. By now we've established:

- He may be finishing school, has a job or an apprenticeship or is studying at tertiary level.
- Or he's a NEET (Not in Employment, Education or Training)—this carries risks.
- He may be making noises about flatting or is already out there.
- His self-care may not be optimal at this stage—this too will pass!
- He may choose partners you find challenging.
- He may want to go travelling.

- His brain is still lagging behind his body.
- He's well up for adventure and risk.
- You're going to have to trust him; have faith in your groundwork to date.
- He's got a life—make sure you have one too.
- You need to stay connected to your adult son.
- He's not looking for advice from you in the same way he used to.
- You get to enjoy the man he is becoming.

Well done on growing the beginnings of a fine young man! The ride isn't over yet—with his frontal cortex still in development—but the bulk of your work is done as he begins to really take charge of his life. It's a time to stay close but not too close and to reflect on your own future as he starts to need you less. What hopes and dreams do you still have for yourself? What sense of purpose? Because living through your son will not do either of you any favours.

He's hopefully beginning to live his dream and your biggest gift to him now will be to live yours. Remember, he's still watching you and learning.

SIX

About men

In the end, that's all any of us wants: to know we are cared about—to love and be loved.

Richard Aston

Boys need men in their lives like trees need water. They need real-life heroes they can look up to and venerate in some way, absorbing almost by osmosis what it is to be a man.

We see the results of this first-hand at Big Buddy because we have the unique experience of monitoring the relationships of hundreds of fatherless boys with male mentors over a number of years (some for more than 13 years). We observe the changes in them in the context of them having a mentor. These changes are largely reported by mothers, who experience the changes in their boys on daily basis. They say things they struggle to get their sons to do are done in a flash if requested by the mentor. Why? Because the boy looks up to his mentor and part of that veneration is wanting approval and affirmation from him. It's pretty simple really.

We believe nudging up against a good man is necessary for boys, because learning maleness is 'caught' rather than 'taught'— it's 'who you are' rather than 'what you say' that influences boys most. We always look to see if a mentor can be venerated in some way—not idolised, but he needs to have something the boy can look up to.

Stable, salt-of-the-earth guys are great. Like most superheroes, these 'ordinary blokes' model a 'can do' attitude that imbues hope in a boy and equips him with skills as he leans into finding solutions to the inevitable challenges he will face throughout his life. That's gold right there!

Veneration teaches through a powerful process of transference. Your son sees qualities in the older man that he wants in himself— that he *needs* in himself. His veneration my lead him to imitate, copy or replicate those qualities he admires in the older man. At some stage, his hero will fall off his pedestal, just a little, but when he becomes 'ordinary' those qualities your son found and gained become his own as he integrates them into his own way of being in the world. That's why ordinary heroes are better than superheroes.

We encourage you to think about the great mentors you've had in your life: maybe your parents, a grandparent, teacher or sports coach. It shouldn't be hard to recall them—these real-life heroes will likely stick out like the proverbial dogs' balls because the truth is they are kind of rare and precious.

Among the largely unmemorable, humdrum teachers that populated my (Ruth's) high-school years, one stood out. He was a young English teacher who took a then radical approach to teaching and inspired some of us into our later careers. Poetry lessons were spent lying out on the playing fields in a circle with our heads touching while we pulled words out of the sky to write poems about teenage angst no adult had ever acknowledged in us before. How cool was that? His reward? He got fired! Too radical, even for the supposedly liberal-leaning school I attended. But here's the thing: inspired by this one creative individual, I wrote the best introductory paragraph of what would become my career: 'The sea at my feet, the wind in my hair, the world at my command!' I'll never forget the look on his face when I handed in the essay and he read that intro—his affirmation of me as writer has lasted me a lifetime.

This is just one illustration of the power of mentors in our lives—we've all got them, and they are worth pondering on and sharing with others, so we get a handle on the quality and importance of these people in forming our characters. The more we understand the power of inspiration the better, as far as we're concerned. Because it matters—a lot. Our task, as we mature and begin to lead the generation coming after us, is to inspire and mentor them into being the best human beings they can aspire to be; to strive for their dreams and contribute their gifts to the world—whatever those gifts may be. Well, in between our day jobs, that is—no pressure!

But seriously, boys without good male role-models are often our 'lost boys'. You know them when you see them. They are usually angry or very sad, have a chip on their shoulder perhaps, are disassociated and unrelational, probably lacking motivation and direction, and possibly into alcohol and drugs at a young age. They are also likely to be sexually active at a younger age. They are a danger to themselves and a liability to the whole community because their sense of self is badly formed and they will show up negatively in all the social statistics—education, crime, mental illness, etc.

That's not to say all boys who do not have a strong male figure in their lives will do badly—many will do OK. Our experience is that most of the ones we meet who have managed to get through father-lessness have done so mainly due to them meeting a good woman who taught them to love and be empathetic. But in our opinion—which we acknowledge will not be universally shared—they will still struggle more on some level than boys who had great men in their lives. They may have more difficulties with authority figures, such as bosses of both sexes, and change jobs more often, reporting things like they left a job because the boss was an arsehole. Or they'll get into personal relationships where they constantly seek approval and validation—never a good recipe for a healthy relationship. The hope is, of course, that they can eventually work through these issues if they become conscious of this hole in themselves—and they find a good woman (or man)!

The other real danger for boys without a strong sense of self and belonging—coupled with other risk factors like drug use and/or mental illness—is that they will gravitate to where they feel wanted and needed, including gangs, etc., if that is where the warmth is. If they are welcomed in and given a place in the hierarchy—something boys love to have—they'll snuggle in, doing whatever it is they are asked to do to stay in the pack. This sense of belonging is a fundamental driver for us all—whether it be joining the local theatre group, volunteer fire brigade or miniature cactus club, we all want to know there's somewhere we can gather with like-minded people who care about the things we value. Somewhere in that field of mutual interest, we feel cared about. And in the end, that's all any of us wants: to know we are cared about—to love and be loved. It's no different with 'lost boys'.

Absent fathers

When Big Buddy is accused of 'replacing fathers'—some of whom believe they have been locked out of fathering by feminism and the courts—we say, 'Hey, when men start taking responsibility and stepping up for their sons, we'll happily close the shop.'

Because the impact of absent fathers on boys and on society cannot be underestimated. In New Zealand alone it is estimated some 15,800 boys aged up to 17 have no active father in their lives.

Father hunger is without doubt the most common theme that emerges from the hundreds of men we have interviewed over 13 years. What the majority of men tell us is:

- They wanted more from their fathers—more time and more engagement.
- Their fathers were either working too much, unavailable or absent, or emotionally detached.
- They particularly wanted more praise from their fathers.
- They often found the attention from their grandfathers.
- They wanted their fathers and grandfathers to engage with them more in the turbulent teenage years.
- They wanted less criticism and judgement and, ironically, more challenges to their life decisions.
- They mostly feel secure attachments to their mothers.

We also meet many men who got great attention from their fathers, both positive and negative, but he was a flawed man who hit them as well—and they're still fine. They are angry he hit them, but they are deeply attached and they're fine. The ones that are saddest are the ones who got nothing from their fathers—no attention, no praise. He just wasn't around, or maybe was around but he was more interested in working on his boat or drinking with his mates. Those men's eyes start filling up with tears when they talk about their dads not showing up at school shows or games.

We do not support physical punishment by any means, but we are saying that emotional neglect from the father is worse. Interestingly, it's often balanced with huge support from the mother: 'She was lovely—did everything for me.' (See 'Mum's the word' on page 227.)

While men have historically dedicated their lives to financially supporting their families—well, most of them, anyway!—being a provider isn't enough. We've heard plenty of stories from men whose fathers were not good providers and have never heard any of them complain about that. They say, 'We didn't have much, but I'd go out and look for mushrooms with my dad or go fishing with him—he was always there for me.' It is ironic that there are so many fathers trying to be good providers but what they *don't* provide is what young boys need most from them—their interest, their time, their engagement. Fortunately, their wonderful mothers often do that for them but it's that male attention they crave most as boys. The saddest people are the ones where neither parent is much interested—they are very much at risk.

So interest, engagement and praise are what our boys most need from the men in their lives—in equal measure. One story that really struck me (Richard) was seeing a 60-year-old Chinese man weep as he told me about his father shaking his hand when he got his master's degree. That was the only moment of praise he'd received from him in his whole life.

It shouldn't be that hard. We encourage every man to seek out opportunities to authentically praise the young men and boys he meets in his life. It's not difficult. And no, they won't become big-headed because of it—but they may become big-hearted.

Harder still for boys is when their father dies, particularly if he suicides. One of our former Wellington coordinators, Andrew Morrison, lost his dad to suicide when he was six. His parents had already separated but his father's death was still devastating. We want to share some of his story here because it illustrates the grief boys go through when fathers are missing from their lives, regardless of the reason.

'My young kid-brain blamed myself for my father's death,' says Morrison. 'I brought a lot of it down on myself and what I found myself living with in later life was this belief system that said there's something wrong with me—I'm always going to get either rejected or abandoned. I'm hyper-vigilant, thinking a bomb is going to go off all the time. The more I start to relax and let down my guard, the greater the risk that I'll be rejected. I was oblivious of things going on as a child and then bang! I learned I had to watch out for jeopardy; be more suspicious—less trusting. I felt I'd be disappointed, hurt or dropped in some way.'

Fatherless boys have layers of hurt, says Morrison, and trust needs to be built so the boy can relax. 'It would have been wonderful if Big Buddy was around when I was a boy. I can still feel insecure at times and wonder where I fit in—I still struggle with knowing how to be in groups.'

Morrison says, even now, he thinks of his father often, wondering what could have been. 'He has a place in my heart but I've had to separate out the choices he made from me—I can't take that shit on.

As an adult, I have a respect for his journey—wherever that might be—and an acceptance that he was confused and in a lot of pain and made the best choice for him at the time, with what he knew. I forgive him and I wish him the best for his peace. I can't hold onto how things could have been.

'When I think about what I'd like from him now, I hope and imagine he'd be really proud of me for becoming the person I have, and I imagine he'd be really sad and want me to know it wasn't anything that I did—he'd release me from that.'

Note to fathers: abandoning your children—however you do it and regardless of whatever pain you are in—is a short-sighted solution. Your children will wonder if you left because they did something wrong; they'll learn the world is an unsafe place; they'll battle to trust other men and struggle to feel secure. This legacy will last generations and we do not believe this outcome is what any father really wants. Reaching out for help when your distress feels unbearable and solutions evade you is the best gift you can give your children. In fact, you owe it to them, because what they need most is a healthy you.

Fortunately, men's engagement in their children's lives is changing and their emotional intelligence is growing with it. Big Buddy programme manager Steve Sobota has interviewed some 260 men over 10 years and he says the general emotional consciousness level of men is slowly increasing overall—especially among the under-40s—and they are much more engaged in their children's lives.

'I think two things have influenced that: a slow change in the way the under-thirties were parented, and then for the 30- to 40-year-old guys, of being much more conscious parents.'

Fathers have a broader role in their children's lives now—a more emotional role—and through that they have a bit more self-reflection: '"Who am I?", "What am I doing?", "What is life all about?",' says Sobota. 'They are expanding from their identities in their work roles—that's been their core historically—into a sense of being able to be a lot more things. Parenting and finding more satisfaction in your work encourages self-reflection and development.'

Certainly the new generation of Gen Y fathers are often a lot more involved with child rearing than men have been historically, and are often actively looking for tips on how to do it. Many have come later to fathering and are still 'boy men' or 'lads'—wanting to be out yahooing with their mates. But becoming fathers makes men out of them; that's how men grow, and it's reassuring to see them slowly move out of their extended boyhoods into becoming great dads.

About men

We are in the position of knowing men really well, having intensively interviewed more than 650 of them as part of our screening process. We have been uniquely privileged to hear about their childhoods, teenage years and adult lives as we burrow into who they are and how they are likely to interact with the fatherless boys we match them with as mentors. Few stones are left unturned during these interviews: What were their relationships like with their parents? Were they securely attached? What were the family dynamics? How was school for them? What shaped their sexuality? How was their first sexual experience? We ask about their relationships with spouses, partners, bosses, work colleagues, relatives, children and friends.

We do these in-depth psychological interviews that go right back into their own childhoods because we need to know they are good men (not saints!) who are able to relate, reflect and regularly show up. We're very interested in how they were raised—their attachment issues—because that informs what sort of mentor they'll be.

In the course of doing these interviews over 13 years, we've learned a lot about men. We support this knowledge, which is uniquely New Zealand, with academic research as we continue to review and shape our screening process, which also involves a police check and doctor's opinion; character interviews with a boss, female relative and a friend; and a psychological assessment. We take screening very seriously because mothers trust us with their boys and we owe it to them all to make sure they are safe and happy.

The other thing of note is that we follow the trajectories of the boys we match, because we stay in contact with them over a number of years. We may meet them at the age of eight or nine, and we're often still with them when they reach 21, so we see the different challenges they face as they grow into manhood.

Our experience is that once we've established trust and empathy, most men are hugely relieved to tell their story—for many men it's the first time they have done this, and it's a big relief to get it off their chest. It's common for men to say at the end of the interview: 'Wow, I've never said this stuff to anyone before—this feels really good. I've learned something about myself. '

Our primary concern is, of course, identifying signals in the overall profile that point to the man being a child abuser, but what we are also looking for is congruence—that their experience is reflected in others' experience of them; that it makes sense in terms of how they are now. For example, we might talk to a man who says he didn't feel loved by his father and wasn't praised, and what we get is that he's trying to please us; and that makes sense, it's congruent. But if we get a guy who we experience as needing approval but he tells us he had a wonderful childhood with a loving father who praised him a lot, then that doesn't make sense—it's incongruent. Flag number one!

Once we've established the guy is congruent and safe, we need to know he's a stable, reliable, good-hearted man who we can rely on to turn up week after week for a boy who has very likely been let down a whole lot in his short life. That's the bottom line. The good news is that there are plenty of great men out there!

Despite the occasional bad press men get, the vast majority of the men we meet are good blokes who have tried to be the best fathers, husbands, partners, uncles, sons, brothers and friends they knew how to be at the time. They've faced hardship and struggle in their lives and know they haven't always got it right; they know they've hurt a few people along the way. But they care enough to want to volunteer their time to a fatherless boy in the hope of giving him a better start than maybe they got.

These men are the heroes who don't make headlines because, according to most press, no one's interested in a dad who reads to his kids every night, helps them with their homework or helps fix their bike. We think it's time we heard more about them.

We know that men feel deep loyalty but they don't talk about it much; even downplay it with phrases like, 'Yeah, I will be there for him [their Little Buddy] until they bury me.' It's a quiet loyalty they show their mates, their partners, their children. A very protective loyalty that for most men goes as far as knowing they would put their lives on the line for their people, if needed.

We also know that men hold grief in a uniquely male way. Grief, and the way it is held, is an important part of growing up for men and can be a shared experience that forms very long-lasting bonds. The ability to feel and hold grief with dignity, respect and caring is the mark of healthy man. Look for it and encourage it in your son.

Many men we meet have done some silly, stupid and even down-right foolish things in their youth. Some are quietly proud of their 'wild years'—some are just embarrassed—but they all know a certain amount of rule-breaking and rebellion in their youth formed the better parts of their character now. The only regrets I (Richard) have heard men speak of is the people they may have inadvertently hurt in those years, including themselves.

Men have a strong sense of right and wrong, accompanied by a desire to 'put things right'—to redeem the wrongs and hurts of the past, even when they extend to past generations. I (Richard) clearly remember the story of one man who was born in New Zealand to a young couple deeply in love but not married. The young woman's father would have none of his daughter having a child, so shipped the baby off to distant relatives in England. The young mother became estranged from her father, moved to Australia and later married. The young father moved to another town. The baby, our man, grew up in a harsh and neglected environment in England with two 'parents' who never wanted him in the first place. He did OK educationally and made a life for himself, but always held the flame for his real parents. In his late twenties, he came back to New Zealand. Coincidentally, his birth mother had divorced and also returned home. Our man searched out and confronted her father—his grandfather—and told him in no uncertain terms the great error he had made all those years ago by denying his existence, and what it had cost him. The grandfather broke down in deep tears of grief for what he had done. Our man found his mother and father and got them together with the grandfather for a very poignant meeting. Much was said, tears were shed and, finally, forgiveness settled on this family. The mother and father were married—they had never lost their love for each other—this time with the grandfather's full blessing, and our man got to attend the wedding of his parents!

His strong sense of rightness, his unwillingness to forget, was the catalyst that eventually healed the wrongs of the past. An impressive example of a real man's sense of justice and healing, and the lengths some men will go to redeem the past.

These generational stories seem very important to men. I (Richard) have met adult men who still feel the shame of a grandfather's suicide, an uncle's mental breakdown or even a great-grandfather's apparent cowardice in war. It's good for men to know their generational stories, to feel rightly proud of the positive ones and rightly motivated to redeem the negative or shameful ones.

Lastly, healthy adult men will always have a little boy in them, a fun-loving, spontaneous and adventuresome little boy full of curiosity for the world. When profiling mentors we often reflect on: 'Where is his little boy?' It's the glimpse of that boy we need, to feel assured he's a healthy adult man. It's the balance between that little boy inside and the adult man that's the key to healthy male character.

Mum's the word

Mothers have an enormous impact on their sons' lives—the role they play is significant and our respect for them is immense. So they get the last word. The many hundreds of mothers we are privileged to meet in the course of our work at Big Buddy do a fantastic job raising their boys alone, and we are humbled by their dedication and complete commitment to their sons, often against the odds. Dads are mostly absent or have died, and money is tight. They have to be everything to their boys.

Mothers generally come to us when their boy is between five and seven years old, saying they feel something is missing from their son's life—something they can't fill. They want a good man to help guide their son into manhood but they know that man is not going to be his father. 'He's got me,' they say, 'but I feel he's coming to an age where he needs more than me.' Mothers often have to get past their sometimes negative ex-relationship to admit, 'Well, not all men are like that—my boy needs a good man.' Something seems to change around the time their son goes to school—a shift in his thinking, where he knows there is a difference between what boys do with Dad, as opposed to what they do with Mum.

There are things women can't do, though we must remember this is an 80 per cent rule; there are exceptions and we've met women who've done a pretty good job at mothering and fathering because of who they are. But in a general sense, men are better than women at teaching boys about risk: about how to take manageable risks and to know when you've overstepped your capacity. We've covered a lot about this in previous chapters but it's worth reiterating that boys who don't learn about managed risk are more likely to be the ones wrapping their cars round power poles or having fist fights. When they hit those perilous, testosterone-fuelled teenage years, they're going to take more risks because of the unfortunate chasm between their desires and their abilities.

Big Buddy programme manager Steve Sobota says there is something about physical play—boisterous play that men and boys engage in—that teaches them about risk and brings them alive. 'I think a mum could do the same thing and it would have a similar result, but there's something else, something extra, when a man engages with a boy like that. Mothers report a difference when their boy is "seen" by a man.

'The relationship with the mother is tight—totally locked in and always will be—but something about a man taking a real interest in a boy helps him develop self-confidence and self-worth,' says Sobota. 'You can see it happening in long-term matches at the Big Buddy Day Out—an annual get-together for our big and little buddies. Some of these matches feel so close it's like seeing fathers and sons coming, which is very encouraging for the newer big buddies who see what is possible for their matches. I think that's why Big Buddy is so successful—because the big buddies realise there can be healing, growth and development in the relationship for them.

'It somehow mends their own relationships with their own fathers or helps them make sense of their own world as a man—it mends some of their own boyhood challenges and traumas and makes them more whole in a way. It's a reciprocal, mutually beneficial, respectful relationship that deepens over time. Mentors get just as much, if not more in some cases, than the boy does. I don't use the word "volunteer" much because it seems like we are building relationships.'

Once a relationship with a trusted mentor is bedded in with her son, the mum is released from having to be everything to him; she's freer to get on with being a mother—however she defines that role.

The other relief is she doesn't feel she has to re-partner so her son has a dad! So many women tell us they are really grateful they can choose a partner for themselves now, knowing their boy has a good man who is looking out for him.

But we don't want mothers to think their only option is to get a man for their boy—there's a lot they can do, and they do. Ours is a male focus because our job is to find good male role models for fatherless boys, but lots of the men we interview report very sweet relationships with their mothers. She's often the gateway for the boy into his emotional world—the empathetic world that she models— and that's a really crucial role. It's not 100 per cent, but generally speaking, mothers are more empathetic than fathers. Many men name grandmothers, aunties, etc., as their foundation stones for good reason.

Our best advice to mums is to get their boys away from the television or computer—they need action, real physical action. They need to throw a spear at a real person and find out they cried rather than watching someone throw one on TV. They need to experience real fighting, so drag him around martial arts clubs until he finds one he likes. Encourage his dad to do more with his son and don't helicopter over them, controlling the activities. Give them some rope and let them figure out their own relationship. If Dad's not around, scan your circles for men who can step up for your boy.

Trust that your place is secure in his heart. You'll always be there for your son and he knows that. Just learn that he needs to drive his own bus at some stage and you'll need to buy a ticket on that bus rather than be the conductor. Same bus—different roles.

Summary

Becoming an adult is a complex task. Technically, it means a person is fully grown or developed but really, it is something we do over a lifetime—we are always growing, learning and adapting to the inevitable changes that happen in our lives. We do it at different speeds—some men shoulder responsibility and 'grow up' early; others stay 'forever young'. But their stories contain similar threads, often including:

- Men—particularly fathers—are very important in boys' lives.
- Maleness is caught, not taught.
- Boys need real-life, ordinary heroes to look up to.
- Without good male role-models, boys can become lost.
- Absent fathers impact very negatively on boys' lives.
- Father hunger is pervasive.
- Boys need fathers to be interested in them, to engage with them and to praise them.
- Boys can blame themselves when fathers leave or suicide.
- Fathers are much more engaged in their children's lives now.
- Most men are good men.
- Mums are bedrocks in boys' lives.

And so we are done! We hope we have entertained you and helped lighten the load that is parenting boys—even for a few brief hours. We also hope you have picked up some useful tips on parenting and hopefully learned something from the mistakes we made. As we said at the beginning of this book, we are not parenting experts—our parenting probably involved more trial and error than considered decisions—but reflection is a fine thing and hopefully our insights are useful to other travellers setting out on the road to raising boys.

Go well, brave people—parenting is the most important, challenging and rewarding work we do. That so many of us survive it is a miracle!

Other stuff to do with your boy, whatever his age

- Airplane viewing at airport
- Art galleries
- Baseball batting cage
- Basketball
- Bird colonies
- Boat trips
- Boating clubs—check out sailing courses
- Boogie boarding
- Botanical gardens
- Bumper boats
- Butterfly gardens
- Canoeing
- Clay target shooting
- Coastal walks
- Community gardens
- Concerts
- Conservation clubs
- Cricket
- Dolphin explorer boat
- Drag racing
- Driving range
- Explore mangroves
- Explore tunnels
- Explore volcanoes
- Feed ducks
- Fishing
- Flying a kite
- Forest/beach walks
- Go-karting
- Go to a car saleyard and take a new car for a test drive. Aim high and try a new Porsche!

- Golf driving ranges
- Historic villages
- Horse-drawn carriage rides
- Horseriding
- Hot pools
- Ice skating
- Indoor rockclimbing
- Inflatable games
- Kayaking
- Laser tag
- Lighthouses
- Local school fairs
- Make up a box containing art and craft supplies
- Maritime museums
- Mazes
- Mini golf
- Model clubs
- Motor racing
- Mountain biking
- Museums
- Observatory
- Outdoor markets
- Paddle-steamer cruises
- Paint a piece of furniture or a shed
- Picnic or fish and chips on beach or in bush
- Pottery studios—check out exhibitions and classes
- Reptile parks
- Rockclimbing
- Rollerblading
- Rollerskating
- Rotate the tyres on your car, check the oil and water, or change the oil or sparkplugs
- Sailing
- Snorkelling
- Speedway
- Split wood with an axe and light a fire
- Squash
- Start a garden—find out what winter crops are ready to be planted, learn about the care of soil, plants and the use of tools
- Sumo wrestling
- Surfing
- Tenpin bowling
- Tenting
- Theme parks
- Train rides
- Tram rides
- Trampolining
- Volleyball
- Walks—check out local walking tracks in your area

- Warriors or other sports games
- Wash the car and tidy the garage
- Water-blast a fence or a driveway
- Wave pools
- Windsurfing
- Woodwork project—teaching the use of carpentry tools; build a birdhouse, a go-kart, a coffee table, a bookshelf
- Zoo, junior zookeeper programme

Acknowledgements

To all our mentors—the courageous men who have shared their stories over the last 13 years.

To the mothers, grandmothers and guardians who have trusted us with their sons.

To the boys, who are a constant source of inspiration and joy to their mentors, and to us.

To our magnificent Big Buddy coordinators, past and present, who engage in the 'magic of the match', working towards finding just the right mentor for every boy: Steve Sobota, Martin Hosking, Dave Burcher, Nic Heywood, Stephen Bell, Scott Savidge and Andrew Morrison.

Thank you—without all of you this book would not be.

Also, to our fathers and grandfathers, who imparted their wisdom, humour and frailties in equal measure.

To our mothers and grandmothers, who did the same.

Thank you all for bringing us into being and for being in our lives.

To our loyal Big Buddy trustees, past and present, who hold the faith: Wally Thomas, Alan Blackburn, Michael Jones, Mike Murphy, Andrew Cook, Travis Field and Mark Talbot.

To the trusty psychologists who helped develop the programme and assess the mentors: Bruce Mackie (deceased), Doug Dunlop, John Bryant, Eric Medcalf, Andrew Jones, Rick Williment and Ric Church.

To the Big Buddy Foundation trustees, who so generously support our work, along with our many funders: Jeff Meltzer, Grant Fox, Travis Field, Mark Talbot, Clare Wilson and Roger Moses.

And to the dedicated support staff, past and present, who keep the engine oiled and running: Tony Holloway, Jude Gillies, Kim Bramwell, Jean Green, Russell Joyce and Tessa Aston.

Thank you all.

And finally, to our wonderful children—'the children of the dream'—Sia, Djan, Lara and Tessa, and our precious grandchildren, Amelia, Charlie and Maxima.

Thank you all for being the wonderful people you are—inspiring, creative, loyal, loving, challenging and heroic. You are the food of our lives. And thank you to Mark and Simon for being engaged, loving fathers—it's wonderful to know our grandchildren are in good father hands.

References

Introduction

Boundless.com, 'Physical development in adolescence', www.boundless.
com/psychology/textbooks/boundless-psychology-textbook/
human-development-14/adolescence-73/physical-development-in-
adolescence-282-12817/

CBC News, 'Emma Watson's U.N. speech on gender equality
prompts debate over feminism, Beyoncé', www.cbc.ca/newsblogs/
yourcommunity/2014/09/emma-watsons-un-speech-on-gender-equality-
prompts-debate-over-feminism-beyonce.html

Department of Corrections, 'Prison facts and statistics: December 2014',
www.corrections.govt.nz/resources/quarterly_prison_statistics/CP_
December_2014.html

Education Counts, '2014 achievement information', www.educationcounts.
govt.nz/statistics/schooling/national-standards/National_Standards

Education Counts, 'Summary tables', www.educationcounts.govt.nz/statistics/
tertiary-education/summary_tables

National Public Radio, 'The teen brain: It's just not grown up yet', www.npr.
org/templates/story/story.php?storyId=124119468

'New Zealand health survey: Annual update of key findings 2012/13',
www.health.govt.nz/publication/new-zealand-health-survey-annual-
update-key-findings-2012–13

NZQA, 'Factsheet # 9: Are there gender differences in achievement rates?', www.nzqa.govt.nz/qualifications-standards/qualifications/ncea/understanding-ncea/the-facts/factsheet-9/

'The science of gender and science: Pinker vs. Spelke: a debate', http://edge.org/event/the-science-of-gender-and-science-pinker-vs-spelke-a-debate

University of Auckland, 'Survey tracks TV habits of two-year-olds', http://www.nzherald.co.nz/brand-insight/news/article.cfm?c_id=1503637&objectid=11510428

Web.MD, 'How male and female brains differ: Researchers reveal sex differences in the brain's form and function', www.webmd.com/balance/features/how-male-female-brains-differ

1. Hush little baby: the first four years

American Psychological Association, 'Is corporal punishment an effective means of discipline?', http://www.apa.org/news/press/releases/2002/06/spanking.aspx

Baby Center, 'Baby milestones: 1 to 6 months', www.babycenter.com/0_milestones-1-to-6-months_1496585.bc

Daily Mail Online, 'Oh S**T! Children really DO pick up swear words like "vacuum cleaners" when they overhear them', www.dailymail.co.uk/sciencetech/article-2611274/Children-pick-bad-language-swear-words-like-vacuum-cleaners-overhear-it.html

Great Fathers, Dave Owens, www.greatfathers.org.nz/greatfathers

The Hanen Centre, 'Does child care make a difference to children's development? Clarifying common assumptions about child care', www.hanen.org/Helpful-Info/Articles/Does-child-care-make-a-difference-to-childrens-de.aspx

KidsHealth from Nemours, 'Understanding early sexual development', http://kidshealth.org/parent/growth/sexual_health/development.html#

New Zealand Listener, 'Let's talk', Sally Blundell, 28 February–6 March 2015

Psychology Today, 'Imaginary friends', www.psychologytoday.com/blog/growing-friendships/201301/imaginary-friends

Radio New Zealand, 'Raising a quirky child', www.radionz.co.nz/national/programmes/ninetonoon/audio/201761727/raising-a-quirky-child

Simply Psychology, 'Attachment theory', www.simplypsychology.org/attachment.html

TED.com, 'Takaharu Tezuka: The best kindergarten you've ever seen', www.ted.com/talks/takaharu_tezuka_the_best_kindergarten_you_ve_ever_seen

TEDxOrangeCoast, 'Daniel Amen: Change your brain, change your life', www.youtube.com/watch?v=MLKj1puoWCg&list=PLaGOzwY0Dq-LDqy61WiaTTEqkpPc4VPgW

Unitec Institute of Technology, *Advance* magazine, www.unitec.ac.nz/advance/index.php/men-in-early-childhood-education/

Upworthy, 'The science of spanking: What happens to spanked kids when they grow up?', http://www.upworthy.com/the-science-of-spanking-what-happens-to-spanked-kids-when-they-grow-up

Zero to Three, 'Early experiences matter', http://main.zerotothree.org/site/PageServer?pagename=ter_key_brainFAQ

2. Stepping out: 4 to 7 years

ADHD Association website, 'Diagnosis', www.adhd.org.nz/what-is-adhd/diagnosis/

BU Today, 'Special Report: The Addiction Puzzle: Could ADHD meds promote future cocaine use? CAS prof says correct diagnosis and medication key to avoiding drug habit', www.bu.edu/today/2013/addiction-research-kathleen-kantak/

ChildrensMD, 'Why do stimulants work for treatment of ADHD?', http://childrensmd.org/browse-by-age-group/why-do-stimulants-work-for-treatment-of-adhd/

Compass Seminars New Zealand, Nathan Mikaere-Wallis, 'Brain development for babies', www.youtube.com/watch?v=-CB-A4awkRU

Daily Mail Online, 'Healthiest children are those who eat the same as their parents', www.dailymail.co.uk/news/article-2319770/Healthiest-children-eat-parents.html#ixzz3zdpwomcx

Dalai Lama Center for Peace and Education, Dan Siegel, 'Flipping your lid: A scientific explanation', www.youtube.com/watch?v=G0T_2NNoC68

Davis, Bryan M., 'The archetypal hero in literature, religion, movies, and popular culture', 11 October 1997, Stephen F. Austin University, http://tatsbox.com/hero/heroques.htm

Dominican University of California, 'An evening with Dr Louann Brizendine', www.youtube.com/watch?v=9Hqwzjz3238

Dr Hurd.com, 'Bullies in school and around the world (DE Coast Press)', https://drhurd.com/2016/01/13/57633/

GoodTherapy.org, 'Are stepchildren at higher risk for abuse than biological children?', www.goodtherapy.org/blog/stepchildren-family-parents-abuse-0409132

HelpGuide.org, 'Step-parenting and blended families', http://www.helpguide.org/articles/family-divorce/step-parenting-blended-families.htm

Hero's Journey, 'The hero's journey outline', www.thewritersjourney.com/
hero's_journey

Huffington Post, Sarah MacLaughlin, 'How to set limits for kids without
harshness, fear or shame', www.huffingtonpost.com/sarah-maclaughlin-
lsw/how-to-set-limits-for-kids_b_4610102.html

Journal of Primary Healthcare, 'New Zealand general practice should adopt
population-based screening for attention deficit hyperactivity disorder
(ADHD)', www.rnzcgp.org.nz/assets/documents/Publications/JPHC/
June-2010/JPHCBack2BackJune10.pdf

KidsHealth from Nemours, 'Sibling rivalry', http://kidshealth.org/parent/
positive/family/sibling_rivalry.html

Kidspot, 'When should my child start school?', http://www.kidspot.co.nz/
article+3934+128+When-should-my-child-start-school.htm

Learning Network NZ, 'Warwick Pudney speaks about boys' education',
www.youtube.com/watch?v=i1TVfvl0ciU

Massey University, 'Fathers: Myths and realities about child maltreatment',
Felicity Goodyear-Smith, www.massey.ac.nz/~wwcppe/papers/cppeip04/
cppeip4i.pdf

McGibbon, Ian, 'First World War: Impact of the war', *Te Ara: The
Encyclopedia of New Zealand*, updated 13 July 2012, www.TeAra.govt.nz/
en/first-world-war/page-8

Mental Health Foundation, 'ADHD in children', www.mentalhealth.org.nz/
get-help/a-z/resource/9/adhd-in-children

MentalHelp.net, 'Cognitive development: Piaget's concrete operations',
www.mentalhelp.net/articles/cognitive-development-piaget-s-concrete-
operations/

New Zealand Herald, 'Is the internet giving us all ADHD?', www.nzherald.
co.nz/lifestyle/news/article.cfm?c_id=6&objectid=11423984

New Zealand Herald, 'Rainbow nation must prepare for change',
http://m.nzherald.co.nz/nz/news/article.cfm?c_id=1&objectid=11531145

New Zealand Herald, 'Should you medicate your kids?', www.nzherald.co.nz/
lifestyle/news/article.cfm?c_id=6&objectid=11462385

New Zealand Herald, 'Superdiversity: Children lead the way as cultures combine',
http://www.nzherald.co.nz/nz/news/article.cfm?c_id=1&objectid=11531743

Nzone Tonight, 'Michael Irwin: Educating boys', https://www.youtube.com/
watch?v=vmHWjCI_inc

Ockwell-Smith, Sarah, 'Why the testosterone surge in young boys is a myth
(and what really causes their behaviour to change!)', http://sarahockwell-
smith.com/2014/06/09/why-the-huge-testosterone-surge-in-young-boys-
is-a-myth-and-what-really-causes-their-behaviour-to-change/

Personality Tutor.com, 'Qualities of a hero', www.personalitytutor.com/
qualities-of-a-hero.html

Radio New Zealand, 'Japanese youth: Dr Dwayne Dixon', www.radionz.co.nz/
national/programmes/afternoons/audio/201773300/japanese-youth-dr-
dwayne-dixon

Radio New Zealand, 'What 3 to 7 year olds need to learn—Nathan
Mikaere-Wallis', www.radionz.co.nz/national/programmes/
ninetonoon/audio/2595176/what-3-to-7-year-olds-need-to-learn-
nathan-mikaere-wallis

Ritalin Nation, Richard DeGrandpre, W.W. Norton & Company Inc, 2000

Simply Psychology, 'Jean Piaget', www.simplypsychology.org/piaget.html

Statistics New Zealand, 'Demographic Trends: 2012', http://www.stats.govt.
nz/browse_for_stats/population/estimates_and_projections/demographic-
trends-2012.aspx

Sunday Star-Times, 'School ditches rules and loses bullies', www.stuff.
co.nz/national/education/9650581/School-ditches-rules-and-loses-
bullies

Today's Parent, 'Is playing with toy guns normal?', www.todaysparent.com/
family/is-playing-with-guns-normal/

Upworthy, 'The science of spanking: What happens to spanked kids when
they grow up?', www.upworthy.com/the-science-of-spanking-what-
happens-to-spanked-kids-when-they-grow-up?c=ufb3

3. The explorer: 8 to 11 years

The American Psychological Association, 'Speaking of Psychology: The good
and bad of peer pressure', http://www.apa.org/research/action/speaking-
of-psychology/peer-pressure.aspx

BBC News Magazine, 'Your answers to 10 tricky children's questions',
http://news.bbc.co.uk/2/hi/8200022.stm

HealthyChildren.org, 'Talking to your young child about sex',
www.healthychildren.org/English/ages-stages/preschool/Pages/Talking-
to-Your-Young-Child-About-Sex.aspx

HealthDay, 'How to talk to your child about sex, ages 6 to 12',
http://consumer.healthday.com/encyclopedia/children-s-health-10/
child-development-news-124/how-to-talk-to-your-child-about-sex-ages-
6-to-12-645918.html

Kaleidoscope Counseling, 'Tasks of childhood: Late childhood development
ages 8–11', www.kaytrotter.com/tasks-of-childhood-late-childhood-
development-ages-8-11/

LoveToKnow, 'Statistics on peer pressure', http://teens.lovetoknow.com/
Statistics_on_Peer_Pressure

MentalHelp.net, 'Physical development: Average growth', www.mentalhelp.
net/articles/physical-development-average-growth/

Ministry of Education, 'Sexuality education', http://parents.education.govt.nz/
primary-school/learning-at-school/sexuality-education/

New Zealand Herald, 'Tips for taming teenagers', www.nzherald.co.nz/nz/
news/article.cfm?c_id=1&objectid=10512161

Parenting.com, 'Talking to kids about sex', www.parenting.com/article/
talking-to-kids-about-sex-21335549

Radio New Zealand, 'Raising a quirky child', www.radionz.co.nz/national/
programmes/ninetonoon/audio/201761727/raising-a-quirky-child

TED.com, 'Gever Tulley: 5 dangerous things you should let your kids
do', www.ted.com/talks/gever_tulley_on_5_dangerous_things_for_
kids?language=en#t-511200

Time.com, 'Early puberty in boys: When should dads start talking with
their sons about sex?', http://healthland.time.com/2012/11/20/
early-puberty-in-boys-when-should-dads-start-talking-about-sex-with-
their-sons/

Thetolkienist.com, 'Tween from Tolkien: 15 words you never knew came
from literature', www.thetolkienist.com/2015/01/19/tween-tolkien-15-
words-never-knew-came-literature/

4. The wild ride: 12 to 17 years

AA.co.nz, 'Teens on the road', www.aa.co.nz/membership/aa-directions/driver/
teens-on-the-road/

AA Directions magazine, 'How fast should we go?', Peter King, Winter
2015.

The Atlantic, 'Body-image pressure increasingly affects boys', www.theatlantic.
com/health/archive/2014/03/body-image-pressure-increasingly-affects-
boys/283897/

Australian Women's Weekly (NZ edition), 'Inside the new schoolboy obsession',
Tiffany Dunk, February 2015.

BBC iWonder, 'Can video games be good for you?', www.bbc.co.uk/guides/
zcs76fr

Brainwave Trust, 'Teenagers: It's not just their hormones—it's their brain!',
www.brainwave.org.nz/wp-content/uploads/2014/06/Teens_its-their-
Brain_A4_WEB.pdf

Business to Business, 'New tools to help parents battle the biggest killer of NZ teens', www.btob.co.nz/article/new-tools-help-parents-battle-biggest-killer-nz-teens

Daily Mail Online, 'Will your job still exist in 2025? New report warns 50 per cent of occupations will be redundant in 11 years' time', www.dailymail.co.uk/news/article-2826463/CBRE-report-warns-50-cent-occupations-redundant-20-years-time.html

Digi-Parenting, https://digi-parenting.co.nz/

Dr Laura.com, 'A parent's survival guide to teenage boys', www.drlaura.com/b/A-Parents-Survival-Guide-to-Teenage-Boys/-153583452250832039.html

education.govt.nz, 'Trades academies', http://www.education.govt.nz/ministry-of-education/specific-initiatives/trades-academies/

The Guardian, '"We have to start talking about it": New Zealand suicide rates hit record high', www.theguardian.com/world/2015/oct/19/we-have-to-start-talking-about-it-new-zealand-suicide-rates-hit-record-high

The Guardian, 'Academic subjects alone won't set every child up for life', www.theguardian.com/higher-education-network/2015/jun/17/academic-subjects-alone-wont-set-every-child-up-for-life?CMP=share_btn_link

Human Rights Campaign, 'Sexual orientation and gender identity definitions', http://www.hrc.org/resources/entry/sexual-orientation-and-gender-identity-terminology-and-definitions

Identities.Mic, 'A major study reveals what happens to children raised by same-sex couples', http://mic.com/articles/92945/a-major-study-reveals-what-happens-to-children-raised-by-same-sex-couples

Mental Health Foundation: 'Quick facts and stats 2014', www.mentalhealth.org.nz/assets/Uploads/MHF-Quick-facts-and-stats-FINAL.pdf

Ministry of Health, 'Suicide facts: Deaths and intentional self-harm hospitalisations 2012', www.health.govt.nz/publication/suicide-facts-deaths-and-intentional-self-harm-hospitalisations-2012

Ministry of Transport, 'Alcohol and drugs 2014', www.transport.govt.nz/assets/Uploads/Research/Documents/Alcohol-drugs-2014.pdf

Ministry of Transport, 'Road toll', www.transport.govt.nz/research/roadtoll/

NetSafe, www.netsafe.org.nz/

New Zealand Drug Foundation, 'Drug information', www.drugfoundation.org.nz/

New Zealand Herald, 'Josh Williams and Derek McCormack: The higher education debate', www.nzherald.co.nz/nz/news/article.cfm?c_id=1&objectid=11481535

The New York Times, 'What is the point of college?', www.nytimes.com/2015/09/13/magazine/what-is-the-point-of-college.html

Radio New Zealand, 'Dr Frances Jensen: The teenage brain', www.radionz.co.nz/national/programmes/afternoons/audio/20168486/dr-frances-jensen-the-teenage-brain

Radio New Zealand, 'Why New Zealand needs more C students, good all-rounders', www.radionz.co.nz/national/programmes/ninetonoon/audio/201772358/why-new-zealand-needs-more-c-students,-good-all-rounders

Radio New Zealand, 'Young adult author, Laurie Halse Anderson', www.radionz.co.nz/national/programmes/ninetonoon/audio/201753058/young-adult-author,-laurie-halse-anderson

Stuff.co.nz, 'Efforts to get more male teachers failing', www.stuff.co.nz/national/education/64375435/Efforts-to-get-more-male-teachers-failing

Teens Health from Nemours, 'Body image and self-esteem', http://kidshealth.org/teen/index.jsp?tracking=T_Home

TV3, 'NZ must address high youth suicide rates—expert', www.newshub.co.nz/nznews/nz-must-address-high-youth-suicide-rates--expert-2015011618#ixzz3zilc4bTT

5. Go west young man: 18-plus

Bottom Line Personal, 'Mistakes parents make that push adult children away', http://bottomlinepersonal.com/mistakes-parents-make-that-push-adult-children-away/

CNBC Europe, 'Jobless youth face crime, drugs, depression: ILO', www.cnbc.com/id/44902803

The Guardian, 'Mamma mia', www.theguardian.com/world/2002/may/14/gender.uk

Healthline, 'Testosterone levels by age', www.healthline.com/health/low-testosterone/testosterone-levels-by-age#Adolescence3

Prince's Trust, 'Youth index 2014', www.princes-trust.org.uk/help-for-young-people/news-views/youth-index-2014

Statistics New Zealand, 'Labour market statistics: March 2015 quarter', www.stats.govt.nz/browse_for_stats/income-and-work/employment_and_unemployment/LabourMarketStatistics_HOTPMar15qtr/Commentary.aspx#NEET

TedxOrangeCoast, 'Daniel Amen—The most important lesson from 83,000 brain scans', https://www.youtube.com/watch?v=esPRsT-Imw8

The Wireless, 'Waiting for the call: Surviving unemployment', Mava Moayyed, http://thewireless.co.nz/articles/waiting-for-the-call-surviving-unemployment

General references

Celia Lashlie, www.celialashlie.co.nz

Father and Child Reunion, Warren Farrell, Finch Publishing, Sydney, 2001

Fatherless Sons: The experiences of New Zealand men, Rex McCann, HarperCollins, 1999

Growing Great Boys, Ian Grant, Random House, 2006

He'll Be OK: Growing gorgeous boys into good men, Celia Lashlie, HarperCollins New Zealand, Auckland, 2005

The Male Brain, Louann Brizendine, Harmony Books, New York, 2011

The Moral Molecule: The new science of what makes us good or evil, Paul J. Zak, Bantam Press, New York, 2012

Raising Boys: Why boys are different—and how to help them become happy and well-balanced men, Steve Biddulph, Finch Publishing, Sydney, 1997; fourth edition, 2013

West: The history of Waitakere, edited by Finlay Macdonald and Ruth Kerr, Random House, New Zealand, Auckland, 2008

What's Happening to Our Boys? Maggie Hamilton, Penguin Group, Melbourne, 2010